COLLEGE KEYS

Getting In,
Doing Well,
&
Avoiding the 4 Big Mistakes

By
Roger W. McIntire

Summit Crossroads Press books are available at discounts when purchased in bulk for premiums, promotions, fund-raising or educational use. For more information, contact the Marketing Department at:

Summit Crossroads Press
11065 Swansfield Road
Columbia, MD 21044-2709
1-800-362-0985
SumCross@aol.com

http://members.aol.com/sumcross/homepagt.htm

Library of Congress Cataloging-in-Publication Data

McIntire, Roger W., 1935-
    College keys : getting in, doing well, & avoiding the 4 big
mistakes / by Roger W. McIntire. -- 1st ed.
    p. cm.
    Includes bibliographical references and index.
    ISBN 0-9640558-7-2

    1. College students--Life skills guides. 2. Universities and colleges--
Admission. 3. Universities and colleges--Handbooks, manuals, etc.
I. Title

LB2322.2M35 1998   378'.198
                                          QBI97-41172

A Professor's Advice
for the College-Bound
and their Anxious Parents

What a break for a budding college student to know in advance what we had to learn the hard way! Oh, the traumas we suffered at registration, the all-nighters, the test anxieties, and the sometimes trying relationships with roommates and friends.

College Keys, written by Roger McIntire, a Professor and Associate Dean of 32 years experience at the University of Maryland, provides an insider's tips and explanations to help today's students navigate their path through college more smoothly.

Prof. McIntire covers techniques for selecting the best college, studying more effectively, developing winning test strategies, choosing housing, and sidestepping social life pitfalls. He also discusses the four big mistakes in habits, housing, health care, and management of time and money.

The book points out the important signposts from investigating college choices to answering the big question, *"What do you want to do five years from Tuesday?"*

The last section of the book is about parents, their worries, and their need to remain a real part of their son's or daughter's college experience. There is good advice here on how to help a student stay the course.

Other books by
Roger W. McIntire

ENJOY SUCCESSFUL PARENTING
Practical Strategies for Parents of Children 2 - 12
(available as book and audiobook)

•

TEENAGERS & PARENTS
10 Steps for a Better Relationship

Look for these books in your favorite bookstore
or order direct from the publisher
SUMMIT CROSSROADS PRESS
1-800-362-0985
SumCross@aol.com

CONTENTS

Preface

Ready for College?

This book is a high school student's guide to working out choices, getting into college, and doing well. It provides a treasure of tips that will save time, effort and mistakes. If you are a high school student now, you are reading this guide at the best time.

> **Don't you wish you had known, back when you were a high school freshman, what you know now?**

Don't you wish you had known, when you were a high school freshman, what you know now? Especially about how to get along with others, about what's important, and how to use your time for what has to be done. At first, maybe the older students told you stories and gave advice—some of it was useful, and some of it was downright wrong. And some advice from older students was designed to steer you into trouble just for their entertainment. But you have learned the tricks of the trade about getting along in high school.

For college, you can know many of the "tricks of the

trade" in advance. By using this book, you won't have to learn all the new things the hard way. It is divided into four parts. To keep up your sense of humor, each part contains a few "Campus Clips" with true stories that have a message from my "Yes-this-really-happened" file.

Part I (Keys to Getting In) will help you sort out the choices, learn what to look for, and ask the right questions.

When you went to high school, you probably didn't have a choice of which school. Now you have choices and the colleges have choices in accepting you. If you could have selected your high school, would you have gone to an easier one? A harder one? One farther away? What would have been your questions about high schools? For colleges you will need answers to those questions.

Part I also gives you effective strategies for filling out applications so you will have the best chance of being accepted. Helpful and work-saving details are presented there.

Part II (Keys to Doing Well) has work-saving tips for both study and test time. You have been doing well so far, so you must have a lot of the necessary school habits. In college, time becomes so critical that a review of your approach to success is in order. This review can give you some tips that save time, improve learning, and keep the grades up.

Part III (Keys to Avoiding the 4 Big Mistakes) has little to do with grades and studies but a lot to do with your college success! Consider this: Most colleges graduate only HALF of the students who go there. Only half! Did the rest flunk out? No. Actually only about 1 in 10 flunk out! The rest are drop-outs who ran out of funds, motivation, or just gave up *even though* they had acceptable grades. Why?

Part III and its survey results will show you the most

common mistakes drop-outs have made, and how you can avoid these mistakes and end up in the graduating 50%! It goes beyond studies and grades to the four big mistakes—mistakes in **(1) Habits, (2) Housing, (3) Health, and (4) Management of time and money**.

These factors are important because the adjustments in going to college include more than just going to another school. The way you live is going to change as you decide where to live and how to use your time. Whether you live at home, on campus, or elsewhere, your life will be more complicated because college will become a bigger part of your life each day than other schools have been. So Part III takes up some of the complications and how to handle schedules, fanatics, friends, and roommates.

> How do you handle schedules, habits, fanatics, friends, and roommates?

Hopefully, you will develop your approach to college with a little extra thought as a result of this book. It's well worth this extra thought because you'll never be asked to look so far ahead in life as when you are asked questions about college. Even decisions about jobs and marriage won't demand the detailed planning and predictions you have to make in college.

You will go to this college or that one, and select this or that to study and, in the process, reject some colleges and some majors, probably forever. At least, when it comes to jobs after college, you can always make a change. And with marriage, well, that's another long story—you'll need a different book for that.

This book asks a lot of questions about your career and your future that require your personal answers. In the next few years, you *will* answer the questions. Maybe you'll be somewhere else when the questions come up again, but you'll decide on an answer with some thought now, or later, or by default.

You might think you should leave some of the questions until later, but when you decide to apply to college, select one, and go off to be a part of it, you make permanent decisions about some of these questions. It's hard to start over.

If you have already chosen a college, you can just skim Part I. But don't pass it up altogether because it can help you understand the choices still to come. It can also provide a good test of your plan as you have developed it so far.

If your heart is set on a particular college, you need to give very special attention to the chapter in Part I about applications. It can help you make your application the very best it can be!

Air traffic controllers often request pilots to, **"Check your present heading."** It's a way to be sure that all the details have resulted in a direction that will take them where they want to go. The questions and answers in Part I help you "check your present heading" and make sure you are aimed in the direction *you* want to go.

Campus Clip
Just Learning the Expectations Is A Challenge

A new student asked me during registration,
"Could I take your psychology course?"
"Yes, it isn't full."
"When does it meet?"
"Monday, Wednesday, and Friday, two to three."
"I'll take Wednesday," he said.

Does It Make Sense to Put Off College?

You've been going to school now for about 12 years and the four years of college loom ahead. But the idea of putting off college, getting out in the world and making money is attractive. Would it make sense to take off a year after high school and work?

Many high school students delay college and go to work instead. They plan to save up for some of their college expenses and sort out their plans. But if saving up money for college is necessary for you, you still need specific information about the college expenses you're working for. Most students I have known who delayed college for a year, told me later that they really didn't know what the expenses would be and the year didn't help their financial situation much. But they did have a better idea of what they were doing when they started a year later.

> Part of the college experience is sorting out what you want to do.

> The problem with the year off is that it has expenses of its own.

The problem with the year off is that it has expenses of its own. Most students with a job right out of high school buy a car, start payments, get a credit card, start payments, buy some things they have always wanted for themselves, and continue the payments. They are not ahead by much after a year's work. So the pitfalls of the year off are cars, credit cards, and getting comfortable with a little money.

Other reasons for delaying college. You may feel you need a little time before college just to sort out what you want to do. This can be a good reason, and it's worth some thought. A big commitment and a great expense can be scary if you are not sure what you want to do.

Another more specific reason for a person to take a year off would be to reach a better understanding of his/her career plans. However, if you are searching for a career, college may be exactly what you need! Most freshmen change their area of concentration at least once while taking their first courses and talking to fellow students in many different fields. So part of the college experience is sorting out what you want to do in life.

The basic courses, which you will have to take whether you start now or later, are there to give you wide information and tell you about many possible careers. And the experience of joining so many people studying in a wide number of fields will inform you about lots of options you might never have considered.

> You'll never be asked to look so far ahead in life as when you are asked questions about college.

A year working a job is a big effort. Before you start, find out just how much money you will need to start the first college year. Don't rely on the advice of others about expenses. Every campus and every student has a different story. Spending habits are different and so are sources of support for college.

How much can your parents and others help? How much effort will you put into looking for support, using the resources and tips in this book? You need the details now.

Call your nearest college and ask for the student financial assistance office. They can answer a lot of your questions about loans, jobs, grants and scholarships now—before you delay college a year, getting a little bit of money that may not be worth an extra year of effort.

There's another option. Work *and* go to college. Most students settle on this option after their freshman year, but some begin college *and* a job right away. The situations vary. You may know some students a year or two ahead of you who live at home, work, and go to a local college part time, or who go off to college and give work the smaller share of the time. Many of my students started this way and most remained with a combination of school and work. So this decision doesn't have to be an all or none choice; the decision can be a compromise.

Since putting off college for a year in favor of a job has its drawbacks, you need to find out more about college—read on....

PART I

Keys to Getting In

Chapter 1

Collecting Information and Taking the Entrance Tests

Selecting a "Good" College

What is a "good" college? One with a good social life? One with faculty who teach well? One with many majors to choose from? One in a nice college town or one in a large city? Everyone wants to go to the best that is available, but which one is that?

The Media, the Hype, and Looking Out for Number 1!

Remember your first days in high school? Remember all those stories, warnings, and advice about everything from lunch to lockers? Some of it was probably good advice as it turned out, but you probably found a lot of it was wrong. For college, beware of similar advice that begins: *"You'll never get into...," "University X is just a party school...,"*

"University Y is too expensive...," or *"The best place to go is...."*

The reputation for academic excellence of your college will be an important part of your résumé for a long time to come. How can you acquire information on the academic quality of the colleges you consider? Average SAT scores can give you a start. The averages tell you something of the quality of the students who will be with you in your classes. Another measure is how competitive the school is. This is usually described as a proportion of the number of applicants compared with the number accepted. Resources noted in this chapter will have information on SAT scores and on how competitive each school is. They will often provide additional ranking of academic quality.

> **Keep the smaller campuses on your list until all the information is in.**

For a particular course, teacher, or even program, the school's reputation may be misleading, but the reputation of the school overall in the mind of the public is important to you.

Colleges are all different, and the rumors and TV-news you hear about them usually only cover football teams, basketball finals, homecoming queens, and fascinating research projects that make up the high-profile news.

New courses and programs that allow students to earn *and* learn in a college's local community, new majors within business, computer science, law, and medicine don't make it onto your local TV station as often as sports and celebrations. Even media ratings of "party schools" and "serious schools" are not very useful. *Your* situation at the college is the important part.

So media information about campuses can be one-sided, and that side tells you very little about the aspects of the college important to you.

Also, the smaller colleges often get less media attention. Large universities with their big football and basketball teams, research grants and graduate programs have larger budgets for all the activities that attract the media. Smaller colleges, with very few post-graduate programs (for degrees and certifications beyond the undergraduate bachelor degree), will attract little attention.

But for you, the small classes and personal atmosphere of a small college may outweigh the hype of the large and less personal campus. Keep the smaller campuses on your list until *all* the information is in.

Which College Is for You?

As you talk with friends, parents, and teachers about colleges, do you feel uneasy about going to a large school, or lonely when you consider one that is far away? How would you feel about going to a relatively unknown school? One with a small, friendly student group? Or would you lean toward a school with a large and exciting campus?

> **You will want information from more sources than just books and the answers to your letters.**

You can begin to sort out the answers to these questions using the books described below. You can add other resources suggested by teachers and friends and begin to fill in Chart #1: College Basic Facts and Figures, like the sample on page 6.

Chart #1
College Basic Facts and Figures

	Ideal	College 1	College 2
1. Size			
2. Cost			
3. Distance from home and travel costs			
4. Competitiveness			
5. How do major programs measure up?			
6. Average SAT scores			
7. Reputation as you know it (Party school? High or low standards?)			

Notice that housing, social life, meal plans, size of courses and other important details are not included in this first chart. These details are usually missing from the published resources that describe colleges. The resources do allow you to get started, and after you have looked up 25 or so colleges for Chart #1, you can add the details listed in Chart #2 on page 14 as you visit colleges and talk to students. Chart #3 in the next chapter will bring all these details together and then you can begin reducing the list.

Looking into all the possibilities can be a real chore. Check your local bookstore for books that list and describe colleges. Here are two of the most popular ones. Be sure to check the publication dates to make sure you are getting the latest information.

> **Be sure to check publication dates.**

• *The Best College for You* published by The Princeton Review (not related to Princeton University) and Time Inc., is in a magazine format. The book lists admission standards, costs, locations, and other particulars of 1,220 colleges.

• The Princeton Review's *The Student Access Guide to the Best Colleges* by Tom Meltzer, Zachary Knover, and John Katzman, Villard Books, New York.

Your library has many other complete sources.

Next, bring up the internet information on colleges. One address to visit is **http:\\www.collegenet.com** This web site includes the option of creating an "Applyweb" account at the site to store your information for applications. You can even use the site to fill out and send applications along with the application fees charged to a credit card.

You might want to use the internet to apply to colleges, but completing applications this way can be dangerous. For example, students are tempted to send off their answers without letting others read and comment on their work. Don't make this mistake. **Be sure your applications are reviewed by others for mistakes in writing, organization, understanding, and strategy. See Chapter 3.**

> Be sure your applications are reviewed by others.

Now is the time to ask your high school counselor for additional information on college programs. Or ask your librarian for sources. Your objective here is to consider a wide list of possibilities. You will need dozens of prospects in order to select 20 or so schools that fit your financial situation, the locations that would be acceptable, and the programs you find interesting, along with particular schools that you find attractive for other reasons.

The main consideration here is to include *all* possibilities. Often the reputation of a college that has reached you will turn out to be wrong when you really look into it.

Campus Clip: **Be Informed About Your Choices!**

Application question: *"Why do you want to come to the University of Maryland at College Park?"*

Answer: *"I have always had an interest in ships of the sea. Living in Baltimore will be a dream come true."*

The University of Maryland at College Park is on the border of Washington, DC—30 miles from Baltimore.

What Will the Expenses Be?

Near the top of Chart #1 is costs. Is college just too expensive? Here's another area where rumors and stories can give you a wrong impression. Although tuition at some schools is over $20,000 a year, the average is under $3,000. Two-year public colleges average under $1,500. *Actually, less than 1% of all students in the U.S. pay as much as $20,000.*

See the *New York Times Magazine* of April 20, 1997 for more statistics concerning college expenses.

It's true that tuition costs do not include living expenses, travel back and forth, or books, etc. But on the other hand, they also leave out financial aid, scholarships, work-study (with pay) programs, and grants. About 60% of college students have some form of financial aid and many more than that hold part-time jobs.

So in this first stage of searching, include colleges

> Here's another area where rumors and stories can give you a wrong impression.

that may seem to be a little bit out of your price range. The expenses may be less than you think. Also, the financial aid office of the college you select may be able to develop a package of grants, loans and scholarships that will bring the cost of even expensive schools down to an affordable level.

What financial aid programs are available and how to apply to them is next.

Information On Financial Aid

Over half of the high school students go on to college, and two-thirds of those receive some kind of financial aid from their college, the state, or federal programs. Close to 6 million students have some kind of help.

Some programs are "need-based" meaning that your family income and expenses must be submitted in order to determine whether or not you are eligible for support from a particular program. Other programs are "non-need-based" and the finances of your family have little or nothing to do with your eligibility.

In your senior year, you will need to check out a few sources such as Barron's *Complete College Financing Guide* by Marguerite J. Dennis (Barron's Educational Services, Inc., Hauppauge, NY, 1995). This book presents many of the financial and informational forms and walks you through the questions one at a time.

The most important form, for example, is the FAFSA (Free Application for Federal Student Aid), a single application necessary for determining eligibility for Title IV federal college support programs and student loans.

The Barron's Guide advises students to apply for financial aid regardless of family income. If denied financial aid one year, apply again the next. Apply early and check the deadlines set by the college or university you select. Don't leave any question unanswered on the form and *don't forget to sign the application!*

Another useful book likely to be available from your local library is *College Check Mate: Innovative Tuition Plans That Make You a Winner* by Debra L. Wexler, Octameron Associates, Alexandria, VA, 1995. This book provides a list of financial programs by college across America.

Also look into the ***College Costs and Financial Aid Handbook***, by the College Entrance Examination Board, New York, which provides details of costs at individual schools, by programs, and with special information on financial help. It also separates need-based and non-need-based programs. You may be surprised to find that many need-based programs have a liberal interpretation of financial need that would include your situation.

> Many need-based programs have a liberal interpretation of financial need that would include your situation.

Ask your high school guidance counselor for other resources. The college financial aid office can provide forms and information about which ones are most applicable to your case. For further information on financial aid, take advantage of the College Answering Service toll-free line, 1-800-891-4599, and the Internet website, **http://www.salliemae.com.**

Letters to Write in Your Junior-Senior Summer

During your junior-senior summer, you need to write those 20 or so schools that are of interest to you. Don't waste a lot of your effort on these letters. This is not the time for a crafted letter listing your strong points or even the strong points of the college that has attracted your attention. A letter similar to the one on the next page will do to tell their office staff to send you materials. **But don't conclude that just because the letter can be short that it is totally unimportant.**

Sample Letter for Information and Application Forms

Get precise address from your resource books or the internet.

Office of Admissions
University of Interest
Interest, AZ

Dear Sir or Madam,

I am writing to request application materials for application to your undergraduate program for the fall of 19xx. I would also appreciate any supplementary materials relevant to financial assistance programs and scholarships. Please forward the materials, including information about possible early acceptance programs, to the address below:

      John Jones
      123 Franklin St
      Hogan, Il   22222

            Thank You,

            John Jones

Do a neat and careful job because the letter may be the beginning of a file the college will keep if you apply to their program. The content can be brief as in the sample on page 12.

Your College Questions

Now that you've begun to develop a list of possible colleges of interest to you, you will have formed additional questions of your own and you'll need answers from more resources than just books and materials from colleges. You need Chart #2 similar to the one on page 14 to put in the details from visits, advisors, and friends.

Friends who have "been there and done that" can be a big help. But they could have had unusual experiences so you need answers from several people. When a college makes it onto your list of possibilities, the following questions are good ones to take on your visit to a campus or when you see a friend who is back from college for a vacation.

Questions for Chart #2

1. How do students and others rate the courses?
Small colleges are more likely to emphasize good teaching and reward faculty accordingly. Faculty at the larger schools are usually more dedicated to research which can be an advantage—they are studying some part of the latest developments, have grants, and hire students! On the other hand, large colleges and universities are likely to have large classes—especially in the courses for freshmen and sophomores.

Chart #2
College Questions & Answers
from contacts, visits and interviews

	College 1	College 2
1. How do students and others you know rate the quality of the courses? What sizes are the courses?		
2. How satisfied are the students you know at this college? Where else had they applied?		
3. How available are advisors to help freshmen?		
4. Are some students thinking of changing college next term or next year? Why?		
5. What options are available in campus housing?		
6. How many students live on-campus; how many commute?		
7. What majors are others considering?		
8. What are the possibilities in financial aid?		
9. How convenient is it to travel from home to campus?		
10. Are there fraternities and sororities on campus? What reputation(s) do they have?		

2. **How satisfied are the students you know at this college?**

   Are they happy with their choice?
   Who else do you know who is going to that college? Where else did they apply? Are they glad they made the choice they did, or do they wish they had gone somewhere else? Why and where?

   > Do they wish they had gone somewhere else? Where?

3. **How available are advisors to help freshmen?**

   Has your friend's advisor been a help in selecting courses and programs? How often have they been able to see their advisor? Was the advisor helpful during registration? Does the college assign special advisors for different majors?

4. **Are some students thinking of changing colleges next term or next year?**

   Yes? Why? Does your friend know anyone who made a change from or to the college? What reasons did they have for leaving (or coming to) that school?

5. **What options are available in campus housing?**

   Most colleges have several choices in housing that differ in cost, meal plans, rules about curfews, coed housing, and quiet study hours. Most freshmen feel they want a lot of freedom but after they have lived with a crowd of people who have a lot of freedom, many select another situation in later semesters.

6. **How many students live on campus and how many commute?**

This is an important question because if most students jump in their cars and go their own way right after classes, the social life on campus will suffer. Even if *you* intend to be one of the commuters, you should look for a college where many students live on campus because they will be the prime movers of campus activities. Also, commuters tend to have jobs that take more hours away from college life.

7. **What major(s) is your friend considering?**

What ones has s\he rejected? Why? Friends' majors may not be yours, but the issues they are struggling with can help you understand the choices. Possibly the job market has become a big part of their thinking as they have proceeded through college years one and two.

It's common for freshmen to follow their interests early on and then reconsider and start looking for a compromise between interests and the practical job market. Many art students (*"I love to draw."*) switch to art education (*"Maybe I can make a living teaching art."*), and many engineering students (*"I love mechanical stuff."*) switch to a business major (*"Most successful engineers end up dealing with more business than drawing boards, anyway!"*). Does your friend's campus have enough majors and programs to allow this kind of switching?

8. **What are the possibilities of financial aid?**

Your friend might not know much about this, but it's worthwhile to get started on where and how to find out. Is there a financial aid office? Does he\she know anyone getting help from that office? What jobs do students have on campus?

9. **How convenient is it to travel from home to college?**
   How does your friend get back and forth to college? Are there any car pools? How do you get around during the week? What transportation to and from the airport is available? What do plane tickets usually cost?

10. **Are there fraternities and sororities on campus?**
    What reputation(s) do they have? What proportion of the students belong to fraternities and sororities? One advantage of fraternities and sororities is their full schedule of social events. But they have drawbacks which will come up later on page 36, so you'll need to ask about other groups.

    What other campus groups are active? Do they sponsor social activities and events? Usually the student government on a campus has a list of groups and their activities. Make a note to ask for a copy of the list. For example, my university lists over 200 groups ranging in interests from computers to biking, skiing, environmental action, political action, chess, community service, and foreign films.

Ask your questions about all the colleges that are possibilities. We'll help you pare down your list in Chapter 2. With your list of colleges and your list of questions and answers, you are ready to put them all together in chart #3 called "Your Composite Chart of Facts and Answers," in Chapter 2. But before we end this description of the first steps, there's one other preparation you need to do in your junior year....

What's all this alphabet soup? In sorting through all
the tests and books about them, the shorthand for test
titles can be confusing. Here's a list of the most
common ones:

ACT: American College Testing (Program
Assessment)

CBAT: College Board Achievement Test

NMSQT: National Merit Scholarship Qualifying
Test

PSAT: Preliminary Scholastic Assessment
Test

SAT·: Scholastic Assessment Test (SAT I:
Reasoning Tests, covers math and
verbal skills; SAT II: Subject Tests, is
a series of subject tests in areas such
as History and Social Science).

Taking the PSAT, the ACT, or the SAT I and II*

I am sure you have received plenty of advice about taking these tests, and this book is not intended as a guide to
preparing for them. Other books are available that provide
practice tests and can help you review and become familiar
with the structure of the tests. Look in the 378.0 section of
your library and check your local bookstore.

What test will you take? That depends on your high school
program. Later, your individual college may require a particular test when you apply for a particular program. Ask your
high school guidance counselor for advice on what tests to
prepare for, when they will be given, and what sources for

* SAT (Scholastic Assessment Tests) is a registered trademark of the
College Entrance Examination Board.

preparing for the test are recommended.

The following list includes some popular books for help on the tests, but you need to consider others to find the best one for the particular areas in which you need help.

Always check the publication dates on these books to be sure you have the latest one and that it covers the newest form of the test you will be taking:

- *PSAT / NMSQT:* (Covers the Preliminary SAT tests and the National Merit Scholarship Qualifying Test), published by Barron's Educational Series.

- *Preparation for the SAT (new test):* An Arco book by Macmillan, Inc.

- *Barron's How to Prepare for SAT I* by Samuel C. Brownstein, Mitchel Weiner, and Sharon Weiner Green. Barron's Educational Service, Inc., Hauppauge, NY.

- *The Very Best Coaching and Study Course for the SAT I,* published by the Research and Educational Association.

- *Barron's Students' #1 Choice* (for the) ACT (American College Testing program) by George Ehrenhaft, Robert Lehrman, Allan Mundsack, and Fred Obrecht. Barron's Educational Service, Inc., Hauppauge, NY.

- *The College Handbook, 1996* (or latest edition), College Entrance Examination Board, New York.

The Appendix lists additional guides. Compare these books with the many other guides available and select one that gives the most attention to the areas that worry you. Reserve a little time in your homework schedule to regularly work with the guide you select. For example, specific practice with the kind of questions on the SAT tests will be the most help. A quick review of one of these books in order to get some "tips" just before the test is better than no preparation, but a quick review will miss a great deal of the help you could get by practicing with one of these guides over a long time before the test.

With your test preparation on schedule and Charts 1 and 2 filled in, you're ready for Chart #3, Your Composite Chart of Facts and Answers, in Chapter 2.

Chapter 2
College Facts: Filling in the Blanks

As the material comes in, you may be thrilled with some colleges and disappointed in others, but it's too early to make choices and it's too early to start using the waste basket. You need answers to all the questions in chart 3 of this chapter.

Who Can Tell You More?

Ask your teachers, your parents and their friends and your friends. These advisors don't have to be people who went to the college you're interested in—although that's best. Many of your teachers may have information about various colleges even though they didn't go there because students have returned to tell them how it went.

Students just ahead of you and recent college graduates may have valuable information for you, also. Before visiting a favorite or trashing a disappointment, ask around for help from those who have been there. **Bring your chart of college questions.**

Visiting a College; Calling Ahead

If you have certain college choices in mind, plan a visit, if possible, in your summer schedule between your junior and senior year. But just driving down to look around can be

> It's too early
> to make choices
> or to start using
> the waste basket.

inefficient and frustrating as you ride around looking at closed buildings. You might want to check out a book on visiting colleges. One is called *Visiting College Campuses* by Janet Spencer and Sandra Maleson. They advise you to call ahead, ask for the admissions office, and make an appointment to see a counselor there. While you have the admissions office on the phone, ask about:

1) Dorms that will be open for you to see. Often in the summer dorms are closed.

2) Special events that might be going on during your visit. Special events may make it difficult to see facilities and faculty. On the other hand, upcoming events might give you a special reason to make an effort to go on a particular date.

3) Mention the majors you are interested in and ask if any faculty in those fields could meet with you.

4) Inquire about starting the process for a *Student Aid Report* while you are there. This report, often handled on a computer, can tell you about the

possibilities for financial help for you. Although described in the books mentioned earlier, this is a good chance to begin the process.

Here's a typical first call to set up a college visit:

Office: *Admissions office.*

You: *Hello, my name is John Jones and I'm preparing an application for the fall of 1999. My parents and I are planning to visit the campus the weekend of the 10th of next month. I wonder if I could meet with someone in the admissions office at that time.*

Office: *I can make an appointment for you but it will need to be on that Friday.*

You: *That would be OK. Is there any special event going on that weekend that I could plan to see, and could I visit any dorms?*

Office: *We have student guides who can take you around the campus and into the dorms. As for events, there's just the pre-season football game on Saturday. What major areas are you interested in?*

You: *I haven't decided yet, but I would like to know more about the possibilities in the psychology program as well as dance majors. Would there be anyone I could talk to in those fields?*

Office: *We will make appointments for you in those major departments and call you back. Could I have your phone number and address?*

You: *Yes. It's area code 777-555-0001 and the address is John Jones, 123 Franklin St., Hogan, IL. The zip is 22222.*

Office: *OK, we'll send you some information about visiting with times and places of your appointments. Is there anything else?*

You: *Yes, could I see someone about financial aid programs? I thought I could fill out the required forms while I'm there.*

Office: *I'll add that to your list.*

You: *Thank you.*

Office: *OK, this will be coming right out to you.*

You: *Thanks again. Goodbye.*

You might also ask about meeting with *students* in majors that interest you. If admissions can't help you with that one, you or someone in your family may know a student who is attending the college you are going to visit. If so, try to set a time to call or see them. Ask them what they think you should see on your visit.

You: *Hello, Elton? This is John Jones, I go to your old high school, Belmont.*

Elton: *Yes?*

You: *Well, I'm going to be a senior this fall and I am thinking about going to Typical University the year after. How do you like it over there?*

Elton: *It's great. I'm having a great time.*

You: *How about the classes?*

Elton: *Well, I'm in Engineering so it's pretty hard.*

You: *Are the classes big?*

Elton: *The basic ones are—the ones everyone takes.*

You: *What is your biggest complaint?*

Elton: *Complaint? Well, just all the traveling; I'm living here at home you know.*

You: *Lots of driving, I guess.*

Elton: *Yeah. If you can, you should get into the dorm. I'm thinking about moving in there next year.*

You: *Well, let me ask you this …* (Get out your list of questions.)

A few calls like this and you will be much more prepared for your visit. During the visit don't forget to bring
along your prepared questions. Take notes while you're
there because when you get home you'll want to update your
chart (see pages 30-31) with the new information.

Questions:

> *"Check out dorms and ask the people*
> *there how they like them."*
> *"Ask psychology person how much*
> *math is required in psych."*
> *"Ask financial aid person about jobs."*

Don't forget
to bring
your prepared
questions
on the visit.

Notes:

> *"Dorms are nice, but noisy!"*
> *"One math course is required for Psych Statistics. You*
> *have to take a math test to see which math course you*
> *have to start with."*

Do a Little Rehearsing for Interviews

Often the college you visit will want you to have a meeting with an admissions counselor. You can't anticipate all
the questions you might be asked but for some you can prepare: "Why do you want to come to College X? Why are
you interested in (chemistry, psychology, engineering)?
What career plans have you in mind? Describe your interests outside of school." Practice some answers to these
questions with a parent or friend. This might seem a little
hard to do but the practice will pay off at interview time:

Dad: *So you're from Belmont. We get a lot of students from there.*

You: *It's been a great school.*

Dad: *I see you put down psychology as a possible major. How did you get interested in that?*

You: *I had a course in it at Belmont and I like working with people.*

Dad: *It's a field that usually requires graduate school. Have you thought about that?*

You: *Yes, I'm planning on graduate school.*

Dad: *Why are you interested in our University in particular?*

You: *The psychology department seems good and I'm interested in the honors program. It's also close to home.*

Dad...

If you have already submitted an application, be careful not to make the mistake of assuming that questions already asked on the application won't come up in the interview. As a matter of fact, most students report that the interview questions were very similar to the ones on the application.

Campus Clip
Prepare for Interviews

I asked a prospective student one summer:
  *"So why is engineering one of your top choices
  for a major?"*
Answer: *"I want to work on engines."*
  "You mean mechanical engineering?"
  "Yes, but mainly the engines. I have a car."

Chart #3: Your Composite Chart of Facts and Answers

When the answers to your letters come in and your notes from visits accumulate, you will have quite a pile of information to go through. Before digging in, start a composite of your Chart #1 (Basic Facts and Figures) drawn from books and internet resources and your Chart #2 (Your College Questions and Answers from contacts, visits, and interviews). This way, after all the information is on one chart, you'll have a good review sheet when the time for the final decision comes. My example of the composite chart is on pages 30-31. A blank chart for your use is in the Appendix on pages 141-145.

> A blank chart
> for your use
> is in the
> Appendix on
> pages 141-145.

Notes About the Chart

How many columns do you need? Probably more than you first believe. My chart has room for only two schools, but yours should have room for up to 20! Most of your local schools belong on your list. You may think you know all about them, but I would bet you'll have a few surprises— especially in availability of programs. Also fees may vary if you are a resident of the state, qualify for honors programs, etc.

The information on your chart will come in handy also in deciding whether to start out at a local school taking the courses required of everyone and then changing later when you need that special training in your major. Ask the students you know at local colleges how their plans are working out.

Row 1 of the chart: Size.

Size is important, but the effect on your social life depends a lot on what your particular situation will be. No matter how extensive campus activities, clubs and entertainment are, social life can still be bleak if they are too inconvenient for you or you don't have enough time to attend. For example, if you plan on attending

> You may think you know all about your local schools but I would bet you'll have a few surprises.

a large university while living at home, working 25 hours a week, and commuting a long way to school, you will probably complain later that there's no social life at the large university.

But if you live in a small dorm or in a fraternity or sorority and have a job on campus, the "factory university" may not seem lonely to you.

Example of Chart 3
Your Composite Chart of Facts and Answers

Question	College #1	College #2
1. Size	Big, 40,000 students; I could get lost there.	Medium, 5,000; Seems big enough to have all the important features.
2. Fees per semester: Tuition and fees: Housing costs Extra costs (special travel to and from)	$3,000 $1,200	$12,000 $ 1,500 Probably $200/ trip
3. Distance from home/ travel costs	Close. I could come home on weekends!	Far. Requires airfare—$200/ trip.
4. Competitiveness	Moderate. Well within my SATs & H.S. record.	Very. This is a long shot.
5. Major options and special programs	122 majors; Many areas in teaching; Every kind of sports you can imagine!	30 majors; Teaching and phys. ed. main ones; good program for teachers.
6. Average SAT scores	1050	1150
7. First reason for going to this college and impression of reputation overall.	Close to home.	Small town. Excellent course quality!
8. Size/quality of courses.	Some very large 500!	Great!
9. Student satisfaction.	Depends on major and living situation.	Everyone on campus. Seems good.

Example: Chart #3 *(Continued)*

Questions	College #1	College #2
10. Advisor availability.	Some students are pretty negative.	Advisors very friendly on our visit.
11. Housing options.	Dorms noisy; many live off campus. Many options for meals. Honors dorm.	Dorms nice. Some rooming houses; not much else. Std. meal plan.
12. Percent Commuters	Over 50%	A few live in town; most on campus.
13. Financial aid possibilities.	Good. Many options.	Some. Very competitive.
14. Availability and reputations of fraternities and sororities.	Make up some of the action. but most students are independents.	Very Greek. Would be a hard decision.

A chart like this will be
a good review sheet
when the time
for the final decision
comes.

Row 2: Fees.

Everyone knows costs for college are high. A harder bit of information to find is how much help you can get. Remember to check **http://www.collegenet.com** on the internet for this information. Most colleges have a financial assistance office that can tell you about everything from campus employment to full scholarships. Don't be discouraged by the stories of how much competition there is for help—remember nearly 60% get help. Often scholarships and loan programs are for specific students—women in engineering, for example, or students bound for seminary, or students in primary education. If you fit in one of these categories, you may find there is little competition for finances or no competition at all! Many scholarship programs go unused year after year because so few students apply for them!

> **Don't be discouraged by the stories of how much competition there is for help— remember nearly 60% get help.**

At state-supported schools, in-state students are charged less than those from out-of-state. This rule applies to more than just your state university. Other campuses of the state university and the state system such as regional and community colleges often have similar lower fees for residents. Starting at a local school can save thousands of dollars.

Rows 3 and 4: Distance and Competitiveness.

These should be available from your first chart, but you may have picked up additional information on travel costs and on competitiveness in your interviews and visits to the colleges.

Row 5: Majors and Special Programs.

You might think that if you know what field you want to concentrate in (your "major"), the other programs don't make any difference. The fact is that you are very likely to change your interests. Over 90% of freshmen change their idea for a major. I found that most students couldn't even name 20 of the 120 majors at my university! They can't consider majors they are not aware of!

But at very small colleges where a wide range of possibilities are not available, you can be faced with such limited choices that you have to change colleges.

A college may have the majors that interest you, but you need more information about them. Talk to students in that major on your visit. Are they satisfied with the selection of courses in their major? Do they feel they are getting the preparation they need for a job or graduate school? Can the

> Over 90% of freshmen change their idea for a major.

department (the office that administers the major) provide any information on how successful their graduates have been? For example, in psychology, 50% or more of the graduates will apply for some form of graduate training. So if you find out that only 20% get into graduate programs, is that bad? That's only two out of every five who wanted to go on. How has it turned out for students from this particular program? How many of their students get into graduate programs in the first year after their bachelor's degree?

In teacher education, many graduates will be working in local public schools. On your visit, could the college suggest a few teachers who graduated from their school that you could call while you're there? Ask these teachers how they feel their preparation served them when they got out.

The other majors are also important because it's likely that more than half of your courses will be outside your major—requirements and electives from other majors. For example, if the history courses offered are so few that no major in history is possible, how complete can the courses *you* take be?

So you want to be able to select from lots of courses as well as activities—what will each school have?

Row 6: Average SAT scores.

This information should come from your first chart of facts and figures.

Row 7: What was your first reason for this college? What is your impression of its overall reputation now?

After you put down your first reasons for thinking of this school, don't forget to bring the reason up later when checking with other people and when you visit. Get some details on your favorite aspect of this school. For example, if it's the honors program, do the honors students have their own housing? Their own basic courses as well as special seminars? Money for their senior project? What's the most frequent complaint from honors students who are there now?

Overall reputation can be misleading. Often a very respected school has a few weak points and "one of the best" won't necessarily make you happy if the courses you want to take are weak. Overall reputations of well-known schools can trick you into making assumptions that are far off-base and set you up for a big disappointment. For example, professionals who were asked to rate graduate schools of social work, rated the Harvard School of Social Work very high even though it turned out that Harvard doesn't *have* a school of social work! They rated it high just because it said "Harvard!"

Rows 8, 9, and 10: Size/Quality of Courses, Student Satisfaction, and Advisory Availability.

These responses should come from your notes on visits, interviews and contacts. How students feel about their courses and about the help they receive from advisors are crucial details other students can pass on to you.

If you are thinking of majoring in history, even an engineering student can help you gauge the general quality of teaching as well as the quality of social life. Faculty are different between majors, and facilities that would impress an engineer are not needed for a history major, but talking to an engineering student is worth the time even if it doesn't cover all the bases you need and your interests are elsewhere.

Row 11: Housing Options.

On-campus housing costs may seem too high at first, But when you compare those costs to living off campus, factor in the benefits of being on campus—no shopping for food, no preparing food, no dealing with landlords about repairs, no commuting, no utility bills, and no problem with leases when you want to go home for the summer.

Also, living off-campus in a private apartment or house makes you more responsible for your roommates and their problems. Everything from their rides to school to their alcohol problems becomes more your problem when you're sharing a private house or apartment.

Row 12: Percent of Student Body Who Are Commuters.

This should be answered in the college materials or when you visit the campus. The number of students who commute has a direct bearing on the diversity and vitality of campus social activities, and can make a big difference to you.

Row 13: Financial Aid.

The search for financial aid possibilities will have to be continued through most of your college years. Be sure to contact the financial aid office at each school and, once you're enrolled, make a note to return each year to the one at your college regularly for new possibilities.

Row 14: Fraternities and Sororities.

Fraternities and sororities can enrich your college life. Many college graduates will tell you it was a central part of college life for them. But the nature of a "Greek House" (so-called because of the common use of Greek letters for their names) and the membership of each will be different.

Some are only clubs for organizing parties—could be fun but the habit can ruin a college career. Others are truly concerned about the new member's welfare and future. Fellow members can help you with advice, study strategies, and questions about majors.

Selecting a "Greek House" from the ones on a particular campus will be another process, if you choose to take part, after you get to college. But a little information is needed right away. If the campus has a great many active sororities and fraternities, "non-Greeks" (sometimes called "independents") may feel left out. If you choose to attend such a campus and do not intend to join a fraternity or sorority, talk to other independents to see how they get along.

Chapter 3:
Applications!

Before Thanksgiving of your senior year you should have applications in hand, so it's time for tips about applying to college. It's also time to select the front runners and start the applications.

Dreams are hard to compromise and first impressions are hard to change. Between these two notions lie the dangers of keeping your list of college prospects too short, missing the best choice for you, or going off to a disappointment that will be hard to reverse. I am certain your dream school has its drawbacks and I'm also certain there are

> **Dreams are hard to compromise and first impressions are hard to change.**

schools that belong on your list which will have pleasant surprises for you when you investigate. This is true of every school your parents, siblings, and friends think is good (or not good) for you.

So extend your list of considerations and remain tolerant until all the information is in. It is extra work to keep "extra" schools on your list. But you need some schools that you really hope for—they would fulfill your dreams—*and* you need some that are good but seem to have drawbacks. And you need some that seem to be out of the running but if it came to them or nothing, you would still consider them.

You could be too pessimistic about yourself and your chances for those dream schools. Or you could be a little too optimistic about those middle-of-the-range schools so you need the back-up schools on the low side also. Take your shot at some schools you think are first for you, but don't eliminate all your back-ups either.

Also, as every admissions office will tell you, there are good years and bad years in the college admissions business. A slow year for a top school can be good news for a student just at its cut-off point. But a very competitive year can reduce your chances and make you glad you had your options spread out to include your local schools.

> There are good years and bad years in the college admissions business.

How do you get from twenty to six to three? Now that you have a chart full of information, you need to weed out a few. It takes a lot of time and money to apply to colleges so most students select three to six of the ones they have investigated. Which ones do you think are the best fits for you?

Advice Before You Start

I am sure you've heard all the advice you want about how to complete your applications, but at the risk of telling you nothing new, let me list a few good tips as I see them from the college side:

1. Review all applications for similar questions that appear on several applications. You can create an answer that will be useful on many forms.

2. List your unusual experiences and capabilities that you want them to know. This list will come in handy when you re-read your completed applications. It will provide a checklist to make sure all your strengths are in there!

3. Some applications ask for a piece of creative writing, such as an essay. Start a creative writing piece from one of your high school assignments or a personal experience. Re-

> **Remember you write best when you write about something you know.**

member you write best when you write about something you know; don't start out to write science fiction if you've never written any before.

Picture the Person Who Has
To Read Your Application

The person who reviews your application is likely to have dozens more piled high on his or her desk. Yours will probably be the umpteenth, so make the unusual aspects of your application very easy to find. You want it to be easy for the reader to find your strengths even during a quick skim of your application. **While attempting to be a wonderful writer, you don't want to bury the punch line.**

Compare the following two answers to the question "What school activities have helped you most in developing your academic skills?"

Answer Number 1:

"Since my early grade school days I have had an interest in computers. The exciting and fast-moving challenges of video games captured my curiosity about the intricate programming that allows such games to work.

"When I moved on to high school, I also moved on to computer programming. I am president of our computer club and, with the help of my high school math teacher, Mr. Exponent, I developed programs for several science projects including the conditioning of frogs."

Or Answer Number 2:

"As a member of our school computer club, I have developed my skills and broadened my interest in computer programming. This year with the help of my math teacher, Mr. Exponent, I have developed several science projects using the computer including the conditioning of frogs.

"This semester I was elected president of our computer club."

The first answer may seem more personal and provide a sense of the student's first excitement with "high tech." But the main points that distinguish this student from all the other applicants are buried in the middle of the second paragraph! The work on computer programs, the individual work with a teacher (who we hope is also writing a letter of recommendation that mentions the projects), and the honor of being elected president of the computer club are the points that are the hardest to find!

The second answer uses fewer words but the important points are presented up front. A reader with lots of work to do could miss the important points in the first answer but is more likely to notice the unusual accomplishments in the second answer where they are not covered with descriptions of your very nice, but very common, experiences. What makes your application different from the rest?

If you have trouble writing in this "pushy" manner, here's a harsh observation that may help. Think of why this reviewer should *turn down someone else* and give you a place at this college *instead!* Write to win!

Just convincing the college to include you will lead you to general comments about what a good person you are without giving the specifics of why you are the *better* qualified, not just equally qualified. The more competitive view will make you put your best characteristics forward.

In the second answer above, you may think that giving a separate line to your success at being elected computer club president is kind of forward and looks like bragging. But if you hide your strong points because you want to seem properly humble, the reviewer may not discover your strong points at all. You don't want to seem to be a braggart and yet your good points have to be put forward. The point of the application is to find out about *you*. Proving you are properly humble is not the point.

> A reader with lots of work to do could miss important points.

If you find it hard to start all sentences with *"I did this..."* and *"I'm the officer in this group or that,"* try imagining yourself as a TV reporter reporting on yourself. Center your presentation on the interesting activities and accomplishments themselves. Instead of using "I" every time, try to report on your experience to break up the "I, I, I," impression. For example: *"Our annual school band concerts of the last three years motivated my study and practice of the French horn. This past year I performed solo parts in two performances. These pieces included..."*

The Dangers of Word Processors and the Internet

You can use a word processor to craft and polish well-thought-out paragraphs for all the general questions that appear on almost every application. The passages can be very handy and save a lot of work, but don't just pop them in unchanged. **The real advantage to these multi-use paragraphs in the word processor is that they are** *easy to modify to fit the college.* When you copy these paragraphs onto the forms from the college, target your answers and convince the reviewers you are familiar with their school and *particularly* excited about their programs.

> **What do you know that is positive about this school? Let them know you know.**

What do you know that is positive about this school? Let them know you know. Let them know what you are looking forward to. Are you targeting a particular program or set of program possibilities? Tell them which ones and why: "The emphasis at Western I-Hope-I-Get-In College on practical business training (in Business Operations 101 and Business Law for Retail Business, for example) would fulfill an important goal in my college program."

So the first danger of word processors and the internet

is that you may be tempted to use the same paragraphs untailored for each college. The second danger is that these tools may tempt you to keep your whole creation to yourself and unreviewed by others. Notice that "Spell-Check" did not catch the disaster that befell the applicant in the "Campus Clip" below. Any proof reader would have caught the mistake.

Your applications are too important to hide from the critical eyes of others just to protect your ego. Show your work to teachers and your parents, take their criticism and suggestions as help, and try to keep your defensiveness down.

Campus Clip: **Always Proofread!**

From an application:
"I know I will learn a great deal about advertising from the asses at the University of Maryland—especially the business classes."

What Unusual Work or Volunteer Experiences Have You Had?

Colleges are looking for more than just grades and school achievements. They hope to create an interesting and active freshmen class that brings a wide range of capabilities and experiences to their campus.

Your grades, test scores, and class rank put your application in a certain group of applications from students with similar records. Now **what will put your application at the top of that group?** Volunteer and work activities are an important part of the application, especially when yours is compared with others indicating similar academic records and test scores! In fact, these activities may be the most distinguishing part of the application.

"So Is There Anything Else You Want to Say?"

Most application forms have a final general question of this nature. At the beginning of this answer present the strongest point of your application in a concrete manner. Then present some new examples of this characteristic of yourself. In the second paragraph present the other points that would make your application outstanding.

There is a balance to be achieved here between repeating material covered in other parts of the application and making sure the reviewer remembers the important points. Lean to the side of being repetitive. Most reviewers have been reading carefully, but they also have distractions and deadlines to meet. What may seem repetitious to you may be news to someone who was skimming part of the time.

Recommendations

In addition to those teachers, coaches, and clergy who would give you the strongest recommendations, also seek out other strong academic people who could give you a knowledgeable and impressive reference. How about your family doctor? Do you know someone who has a degree from this school? A recommendation from a graduate of the school can be very helpful. It is not necessary to use the same people for references for all the applications.

Do you know someone who is on the faculty of a university or college? Or someone who was a leader of a particular activity or event that you were both involved in. Possibly they will be able to speak to a particular quality you have ("I'll ask my soccer coach because I was made captain, and he can tell them about my leadership abilities!").

If you feel the person would not know you well enough, you might ask if they would like to talk with you before they write the letter—a little informal interview. Many people will write a stronger letter after a recent personal contact.

> A recommendation from a graduate of the school can be very helpful.

The most common mistake student applicants make concerning recommendations is to delay asking people to write a recommendation until only a little time is left. Then the letter writer is hurried by a deadline and may write a less thoughtful letter as a result.

The second most common mistake is to neglect telling your letter writer what you hoped they would write about.

When you ask someone to write a letter of recommendation, be sure the person knows what you hope will be covered in the letter. It's too important to assume they will know why you asked *them* in particular. You can't dictate to them of course, but be sure they know the topic(s) you hope they will address.

Campus Clip:
Choose Your References Carefully!

"I feel Robert will do very well in college on and off the field. His high school grades are a little low, but I believe that is due to football injuries. As his coach, I am sure of it."

Before You Mail Your Application

All of us who write hesitate to let someone else criticize what we've done. You've read it over, so why not get it in the mail? The reason is that it's hard to see the mistakes in your own work. You know what you were driving at, so they will too, right? Not necessarily.

Ask someone to read your application while you stay near by. Don't run away just because it's painful to stay. Observe *yourself* carefully. If you feel the urge to explain something and do a lot of talking to be sure they get it, then it needs more work. You won't be there to do any explaining when the admissions office first reviews your application. It has to stand on its own. Take notes on what you had to explain so that the explanation can be added to the application when you edit.

For more details on applications to college check *College Applications Made Easy* by Patty Marler and Jan Bailey Vlk, VGM Publishing Horizons, Lincolnwood, IL, 1997.

Chapter 4

The Long View of College Majors and Life Careers

When the Offers Start Coming In

Having that first offer in hand is a great relief. You may feel tempted to call or write immediately and "get it all nailed down"—especially if this college is one of your first choices.

But before you make that commitment, ask yourself some questions about *the other schools* that you haven't heard from yet: Is there any reason you would select one of these other schools if you had the chance? If their financial assistance turned out to be better? If the housing selection was better? If other students you know elected to go there?

> Take the time your first college has allowed you to keep the options open for a few days.

If any of these reasons come to mind, take the time your first college has allowed you to keep the options open for a few days. Don't be rushed by offers made before deadlines.

Students often feel pressured to "get this wrapped up," as if they feel the offer could be withdrawn ahead of time somehow so they had better take it quickly. If you are worried about losing out, call the admissions office and ask how long you have before you must notify them of your decision.

When you have several difficult choices and specific questions are still unanswered, a second visit to these schools is not unreasonable. For example, in addition to checking out your housing assignment, you might want to talk to faculty at each school.

Now that the choices are clear, it might be a good time to go back to those who gave you advice on your first selections and applications. With these choices, what factors would be most important to people who have gone to one of these schools?

The Big Decision

With all the information in, the visits done, and everything talked over, you have to choose. Just before you take this big step, review the reasons you had for starting this college search in the first place.

Did you, most of all, hope to get out on your own, make new and lasting friendships? Did you, most of all, want to study a certain subject? Did you, most of all, want help in choosing a future career? How do the answers to these questions fit with your final choice?

If independence and new friends were a top priority, a large school close to home would have to have a lot of new-found advantages to make up for being too close and too impersonal to make either goal likely.

If a certain major was your goal, a school would have to have a lot to make up for a weakness in the area you wanted.

And, if you wanted to try out lots of subjects, a small school with limited choices would have to look very good in other ways to make up for the lack of choices.

But after all this agonizing, remember that about 50% of college students change colleges along the way, and that's always an option if your needs change. See "Changing Colleges" on page 110. Many students plan a start in one college as good preparation for a finish in another.

> About 50% of college students change colleges along the way.

And speaking of finishing, Part II will present some tips to make that effort more fun and more productive.

Should You Decide On a Major Now?

In four years of college, you will accumulate 120 credits or more—15 each semester for 8 semesters. Of those, 30 or 40 will be in your major field of concentration or "major," for short. The other 80 will be credits for required courses in English, math, history and so on. Some of the 80 may make up a "minor"—a group of courses in one area but not enough to be your major field of concentration.

Some schools use a different system of assigning credits, and some don't use "semesters" to break up the academic year. So you may have to translate my example using the common semester system to another if you're attending a school on a different system.

The number of credits required for a major will vary with colleges and with majors at the same college. For some programs, such as engineering, the required courses are so numerous that you have to get started on your major right away. But for most majors and at most colleges, you will not need to declare a major in your freshman year. Nevertheless, while you are exploring possible majors, you need to put some options on the list in order to select your first courses.

> **For most majors and at most colleges, you will not need to declare a major in your freshman year.**

For example, if psychology is on your list of possible majors, and Psychology 100 is one of the courses that would fulfill your social science requirement, then selecting Psych. 100 would help you decide and fulfill a requirement at the same time.

You may also be required to take a science course that includes laboratory time. If you are considering a biological science as a major, taking a botany or zoology lab course instead of physics could serve two purposes: It fulfills the lab science requirement and gives you a better understanding of your possible major.

Almost all freshmen have a change of mind about their major early on and *more than half of the students at most colleges change majors* later, at least once. *Nearly half* change *more* than once!

In most cases this is not a serious mistake that will "delay" graduation. In the first few semesters, many of your courses will be basic requirements needed for any major and they will all count. And courses taken while pursuing one major can be used as a minor subject, if one is required.

Also, the courses of a rejected major can fill in other requirements you would have needed anyway.

Your four years will have room for some electives (courses you choose outside of your selected program) and some of your major-now-rejected courses can be designated as electives. The reason you took a course and the way you "use" a course in your program (whether you call it part of your major, an elective, or part of the fulfillment of a requirement) can be changed later.

A false start on a major may seem wasteful—you have taken a course or two you would not have taken if you had gone straight to major number two. But remember you also have choices about how many courses you take each semester as well as which ones. Some colleges may have policies regarding number of course hours—especially for freshmen. Ask the registrar at the college you select if there are any such policies that may affect you.

You need to average 15 credits per semester but you could take fewer at first and more than 15 later, or you could take more than 15 later to make up for a course "wasted" early on.

Keep in mind no one is insisting you do it all in four years—at least no one at the college. At home, you-know-who may have an opinion about that!

> **Almost all freshmen change their mind about their major early on.**

Your college will have career counselors available. They can help you collect information on the majors and the jobs and careers possible with each. Don't make the mistake of assuming you know all the majors that would interest you— no one knows that much. My university has over 120! Also, you may be surprised how much math and statistics psychology requires or how much chemistry botany requires. Talk to these advisors at the beginning. They can be a great help.

A career counselor's most common complaint is that students put off coming in until they are college juniors or seniors and then say, *"Here's what I have taken. What job can I get?"*

The tragedy in this wait-until-later approach is that if only the student had taken this course or that, this minor instead of that one, or had known about this other related major, he or she could have had a much better résumé and a much better college education.

Now three or four years and many thousands of dollars down the road, the student finds out that a better way was missed! Do you know the choices? Do you know what you can do with a degree in Agronomy? Linguistics or Social Studies? Explore the possibilities now.

Campus Clip
Do You Know What the Major Is About?

From my I-swear-it's-true file of interviews with students who said they were interested in psychology:
   "I know it's a big field, but can't I just stick with the future part?"
   "Future part?"
   "You know, palms and stuff like that."

Note: The psychology program does not train palm readers or "psych*ics*."

Career Choices (Or, What Do I Want
To Do Five Years from Tuesday?)

It seems like a long way from your freshman year to graduation, but it's a much longer time from graduation to retirement! The best advice on careers is to talk with people in the careers you have in mind. You want to be a sociology major? After graduation you will be a sociology major *doing* what?

> A career counselor's most common complaint is that students put off coming in, then say, "Here's what I have taken. What job can I get?"

For many majors, the majority of graduates are scattered in many careers. Ask an advisor in your prospective major department about the jobs graduates from that department have. Call some recent graduates.

Many fields—especially those in the social sciences—require an advanced degree after college in order to advance in the field. Do you want to go on to graduate school after college? In psychology, for example, about one-half apply to graduate school somewhere and about one-third of the graduates complete some graduate training.

> You will want to know about the typical days of a particular career.

You will want to know about the typical days of a particular career. Lawyers spend very little time making the dramatic courtroom statements you see on TV. Doctors spend a lot of time on paper work and usually complain about it. Psychologists have a variety of jobs from industry to hospitals to public schools. You would be amazed how many successful engineers advise students, "Take as many *other* courses as you can!"

Planning Some Options: A student of mine who was an excellent basketball player had little interest in picking out a major. He said he was going to be a pro player and didn't really care what major he had.

I asked, *"How many college players make it in the pros?"* He said he knew that very few made it, but he was really good.

> *"But what if you have an injury or just get edged out by other players?"*
> *"I love sports. I'll open up a sports store!"*
> *"Well, It's nine on Tuesday morning. What do you suppose a sports store manager is doing right now?"*
> *"Selling."*
> *"At nine on a weekday morning?"*
> *"Well, if there aren't any customers, he's probably fixing up the shelves or ordering stuff."*
> *"And working on the books, getting some advertising ready, finding out about the latest products?"*
> *"Yeah, stuff like that."*
> *"Is that what you want to be doing five years from today?"*
> *"Well, I don't know, maybe."*
> *"So maybe a business major is something to look into?"*
> *"I could take a course."*
> *"Now's the time to find out if you would like it, and now's the time to get the education to do it."*
> *"I guess. I hope to make it in the pros."*

"Yes, but you are in college now and, at the most, only part of your life will be in the pros."

While you're thinking about college, think about the typical day in the careers you have in mind. It's important to think about not only what you want to *be* but also of what you want to be *doing!*

PART II

Keys to Doing Well

Chapter 5

Tips About Courses, Credits, and Hours

What Credits and Hours?

"Credits" and "credit hours" are sometimes used interchangably. The confusion probably began when credits were assigned to courses partly on the basis of how many hours the course met each week.

A course that consists of three one-hour lectures per week (for example, History 101 might meet Monday, Wednesday, and Friday at 1 pm) would be a three-credit course. A person with a 15-credit program for the semester probably has about 15 class-hours to attend each week. I say "probably" because some courses will not work out quite this way. A chemistry course, for example, could be four credits with only two lecture hours but with four lab hours per week giving you a total of six hours in chemistry class each week for only four credits.

The maddening part of the first few days of college is

that you are asked to make important decisions in a confusing and rushed situation. What classes should I take? What times are available? How many credits would be best? And hurry because classes are filling up! Even when registration is computerized and done by phone, some planning ahead will make decisions easier.

While there's still time, take a moment now in a more calm situation to get a few priorities straight.

What Courses?

In most colleges, you need to average 15 credits each semester to graduate "on time" four years from now. But the beginning is not a good time to try to get ahead of this average. It *is* a good time to watch out for your own contentment and happiness with what you're doing. And for most students it's *not* a good time to get *all* the requirements "out of the way."

Working on required courses early provides you with information about other possible majors and gives you the basic courses you need, but you need to be sure some of your freshman program has special interest for you. Look at this sample schedule:

English Composition for 3 credits
Astronomy for 4 credits
Art Appreciation for 3 credits
History for 3 credits

This adds up to 13 credits. It's a reasonable program; a little short of the 15-credit average you'll need in the long run, but in your first semester a light load may be an advantage. Yet this sample program has some disadvantages.

If you are interested in, say, the animal and plant world and you have a second interest in psychology and how people act, the 13-credit schedule described above has some drawbacks. **First-year students need to look out for number one!** How will your motivation stay up if all your courses fulfill requirements, but none of them speak to a current interest?

For the person who may possibly major in psychology later, how about delaying the art appreciation course or the history course and taking the favorite subject just to keep morale high? And for the student with interest in the natural world, how about a botany or animal behavior lab as a morale-booster instead of astronomy?

> You need to be sure some of your freshman program has special interest for you.

One student described her schedule to me this way:

"I sometimes think about it in terms of a dinner. You need your main entrees (major courses) and your vegetables (general requirements—English, history, science, etc.). But you also need a dessert—courses you elect because of a current interest you have! I treat myself to a dessert!"

Many "main entrees" and "vegetables" can become as good as "desserts" with a good instructor. The reputation of a teacher should be an important factor when you have a choice. Talk to fellow students about their experiences with the different instructors. Students majoring in the instructor's department are often good sources of advice.

A Typical Week

The choices of times will be limited by class schedules and your other commitments. And you may have to leave time open for a job. But don't squander your best time of day. When do you work best? Are you a morning person? Afternoon? Or are you best in the evening when all the scheduled events are over? Developing a rough schedule for a typical week, like the one presented on the facing page, can give you a good perspective on questions that come up in a hectic registration line.

If the science lab is likely to be a tough course for you, try to schedule that lab at *your* best time. And plan to keep some of your best hours for study time.

The trap closes when you use all your best time for personal time: "I'm never good for much before noon. I might as well be in class!"

This plan is a mistake. To avoid this mistake, make out your week's schedule *before* you register. Highlight the best times of the week for you and the events that you would hate to miss.

> **The trap closes when you use all your best time for personal time.**

A roughed-in schedule like this will help you at registration time when choices are presented for immediate answers. Of course you'll have to compromise, but at least you will know what you want. The 9 to 12 and 1 to 5 slots add up to 35 hours each week and you will probably have classes about 15 hours per week. So there's plenty of room for errands, study time and job hours. The point is to know your best times and use them to your advantage.

TYPICAL WEEK

DAYS:
Mon. Tues. Wed. Thurs. Fri. Sat.

TIMES:

6:00 a.m.   A R E   Y O U   K I D D I N G ? ? ? ?

8:00 a.m.   Not a morning person, best time for laundry, cleaning up, other chores.

9 - 12 noon   OK for classes, particularly interactive ones, labs, discussion sections. Fill in non-class hours with serious study time.

Tues- Thurs mornings could be part-time job.

12 noon   I need my lunch; don't want to fill up this time and miss lunch with friends.

1 - 5:00   Best class time; fill in non-class hours with serious study time.

6:00 p.m.   Need this time off for dinner and social stuff. You miss everyone in the dorm if you fill this time.

8:00 p.m.   Could be a class time on some days—not every day. This should be goof-off time some days.

10:00 p.m.   Good study time for me.

12:00 mid.   Not good for me.

2:00 a.m.   A R E   Y O U   K I D D I N G ? ? ? ?

Drafting a rough schedule such as the one above
can make registration day a little easier.

Chapter 6
Doing Well is a "SNAP"!

The letters in SNAP can remind you of the basics that will focus your efforts and pay off in grades.

Show Up. The "S" in SNAP stands for **Show Up.** The first symptom of a student getting ready to fail a course is that he starts cutting class. And almost all students who drop out begin the downhill slide by cutting classes.

We all know you are supposed to go to lectures, labs and discussion classes, but many students rationalize missing them, and they *always* end up the worse for it.

The first rationalization is: "They don't cover anything new in class."

Many students will reason that if the class topics are covered in the book, why go to class? In the unusual situation where class seems like "only review," the instructor, even when not presenting new material, guides you to what is important and gives you a realistic view of how fast you should be moving along.

While there are moments when a class and its reading materials are the same, much of the material presented in class is not quite the same. The examples used will be different from the readings, and the manner of organizing the material will also be different. In most cases totally new material not in your readings will be presented. Often teachers will make test questions using the particular example from class.

> The examples used in class will be different from the readings.

Don't be taken in by the notion that nothing beyond the reading assignments is presented in class; it is.

The second rationalization is: "I already know what they are going to do."

As every "street-wise" student will tell you, no college course ever runs exactly as announced on the first day. Things change. Dates for quizzes and exams change due to weather, readings change, labs are rescheduled, and professors get behind in lectures. Announcements are made, and there are always some students who cut class and then say, *"Oh no! The test is today?!!"*

The third rationalization is: "Attendance is not required."

Some instructors may say that attendance is not required, but they still contribute their time and effort to the class. If you don't put in yours they will notice and you could suffer.

Show up. Show up for the newest material. Show up for the information on the latest schedule of the course events.

Show up for guidance through what is important. Show up to keep pace with the course. Show up to give the right impression. As Woody Allen said, "Eighty percent of life is just showing up!"

And show up occasionally at the teacher's office hours— that's what they are for. You will get to know your instructors and they will get to know you and your interest in the class.

Campus Clip: **Show Up!**

One student arrived at a final exam scheduled with several other classes in a large auditorium:

"Where's the Psych. final?" he asked me.
"They're all psych. finals. Which professor do you have?"
"Ah, I don't remember his name."
"But it was a man?"
"Yes."
"Well, there are only three in here today. Was his name Smith?"
"No, it was a more complicated name than that."
"Must have been Johnson."
"No, I don't think so."
"Only one left, McIntire?"
"That's it!"
"I'm McIntire."
"Oh, well...ah...I've been sick a lot."

Take Notes. The "N" in SNAP stands for **Notes!** "Take notes" is a bit of advice you would think every student knows, but when you look around in your college classes you'll see many students who evidently think they can remember a class from now until finals without notes. Or they must think there's nothing to write about! This error is most common in non-lecture classes. It may be harder to organize notes in a lab or discussion class, but the need is just as crucial. It keeps your attention on the class, it gives you practice with the material, and it's a valuable record of what you need for tests.

What to write down in class. You've been told about taking notes since the beginning of high school and now you need that habit more than ever. **If you have trouble in this note-taking area, try these five rules to get you going:**

1. Write down anything your instructor writes down on the board.
2. Write down anything that sounds like a definition.
3. Write down all examples and illustrations the instructor describes.
4. Write down all lists and titles mentioned.

The Crucial Rule Number 5! Before bed tonight, copy your notes over into real sentences translated from your shorthand.

> Some students evidently think they can remember a class from now until finals without notes.

Don't fall for the notion that your own shorthand will always make sense to you—it won't. And the additional advantage in copying your notes is that you will add details that didn't make it into your notes from class but can be added now while you still remember.

> Make your "good notes" before bed on the day of class.

When a student misses a class and wants to borrow someone's "good notes," what do they mean by "good?" They mean notes that are readable in English without secret codes that are soon forgotten even by their creator. Make your "good notes" before bed on the day of class.

To gain another advantage to copying your notes, put one set in a separate notebook so it will be a back-up if you lose the others.

 Use Active Studying. The "A" in SNAP stands for **Active!** The answer to the problem: *"I Can't Study More!"* is *"Just Study Better!"*

Parents always hope their sons and daughters will "work hard" in school. The "work hard" idea is good advice but by itself leaves out the specifics. Successful work shows up in grades if the student knows how the "work hard" idea is turned into active practice; not just staring at pages, but reading aloud; not just "trying to remember," but talking to others about the work, drilling important concepts, rewriting notes and important material, and drawing new diagrams or tables that organize facts differently. That's how the idea of "work hard" becomes successful learning and great grades!

I never had a student fail a course who had *study* notes! Failure comes from lack of effort in studying.

You would think that this would be obvious enough, but look around you during those first weeks, and you will see lots of students just staring at their work. Many of them brag, *"I 'got through' a hundred pages last night!"*

Too bad *"How many pages did you get through?"* will not be a question on the test!

Try the following experiment:

Pick out a favorite magazine in which there are two articles or stories you have not yet read. Read the first story to yourself in your usual way. Find someone to listen to your report of the story or article and tell them all the detail you can remember—who wrote it, who was in it, what was going on, conclusions reached and so on.

Now go back to the magazine and read the second article or story. This time, stand up and read out loud, with good emphasis and inflection—to the wall if necessary. Now find a person to listen to you report all the details you can remember of who, what, and where.

> Too bad "How many pages did you get through?" will not be a question on the test!

By the end of the second report, you will notice how much more you remember of the second story. As one student put it to me, *"Well, of course, I remember that one. I remember what I said!"*

For learning and changing habits there is no substitute for active practice. On your vacation, stare at pages in a novel while lying on the beach if you enjoy it, but if it's for learning, "work hard."

When I was faced with learning the history of psychology as presented in a senior course, I laid out a chart 4 feet wide to organize the various trends and movements across the centuries. The chart had little red arrows between names of persons who disagreed with each other's theories, green arrows for those who agreed and yellow for those influencing a theory. The vision of that active studying is still with me today.

"Doing" College: Reading assignments often lead the student to the mistake of leaving out the *doing* part of learning. Many of my students have said, *"I can't believe I did poorly. I went through (stared at) all the material for the test!"*

If you only read it (not really actively practice) and never use it, it will be gone soon. If reading is the assignment, take reading notes—preferably on cards with a list or set of facts on each card: Three people who studied a particular topic; two experiments that proved this point or that; four reasons for the war of...; five factors of water pollution.

"Never turn a page without writing something," should be the rule. The rule has several advantages:

1. **Note cards become a source of motivation** because they are a concrete product which can give you a feeling of accomplishment.

2. **Note cards provide bench marks of progress** that allow the student to pick up at the right place after an interruption. It's surprising how much studying is done in small sessions of only a few minutes between interruptions by phone calls, snacks, and chores. Without the note cards, most of us start again at the same place we started before. With the cards, we have a record of where we are and we can move on to new material.

3. **At review time**, the work is condensed as notes,

maps, tables, and drill sheets guaranteeing the right material will be memorized. You can avoid the misery of thrashing madly through a pile of unorganized material.

For more help on study strategies, consider *Toolkit for College Success* by Daniel R. Walther, published by the Wadsworth Publishing Company in Belmont, CA. Wadsworth has a series of great study books for college students from freshmen to seniors.

| **P** | **Plan Ahead.** The "P" in SNAP stands for **Plan ahead**. |

The only thing you get *for keeps* is your time, and the only satisfaction will be in *how you spend your time*. So what to do with college time?

Everybody needs "play and party time." You can't plan every minute you have, but you need plans just to keep the priorities in order. All your time should count for something!

You can plan ahead by listing all the tasks that need to be accomplished in the next week (or day or month). Then prioritize the tasks and schedule them in your calendar of other events.

A pocket calendar can help keep your planning on track. You don't need a note for every hour of every day, but a few reminders can save a lot of trouble.

Examples of entries might be:

"Chemistry quiz Thurs., save Wed. afternoon for review."

"Check with lab partner about num-

> You need some plans just to keep the priorities in order.

bers from last experiment—start lab report"
"Special dinner at dorm tonight."
"Confirm airline reservation by this date."
"Two midterm exams on Friday—keep this week open!"

Your plans don't have to be unchangeable. Even if you don't follow your planned schedule to the letter, the exercise of laying out the priorities and determining how much time is needed for each task will put you on track to getting it all done.

Chapter 7
Remember Good Test-Taking Strategies

Make Up the Test

After you have done all the "snappy" things, showing up, note-taking, active studying, and planning, you may still feel anxious about the tests.

One effective exercise is to make up your own version of the test. The process will make you think of what is important, and how to organize the important points into test questions. Then you can develop answers to these questions. Test-making will reduce your fear of surprises. Even with the right kind of studying, you will need this exercise to gain confidence. Try to make it as similar as possible to the one expected.

> **Test-making will reduce your fear of surprises.**

Students who practice this exercise often report to me that more than half of their questions were the same as the ones on the teacher's test! With those questions answered in advance, students can more easily remember their answers and go quickly to those other questions they did not anticipate.

Strategies During the Test

Here are some procedures to keep you moving ahead without panic during objective and essay tests:

During objective tests:
Certainly every student intends to answer each question on an objective test, but very often items go unanswered. Since questions left blank are scored as wrong, this is a big mistake. When you are not completely confident that you know the answer, take the following steps:

1. Read the stem one more time. The stem is the first part of the question preceding the choices.
2. Eliminate options you know are wrong.
3. Select a final answer; guess if necessary.

You might object to this approach because of the guessing when two or more choices or left. Actually, there are few occasions when you should avoid guessing—even when the instructor says grading will penalize for guessing. Such adjustments in scores assume random guessing such as predicting that you can get one out of four answers to four-choice questions just by chance. Therefore a score of 25% indicates zero knowledge.

> On most occasions, your guessing is not random.

But on most occasions, your guessing is not random. You will eliminate some answers and your guess is improved to one out of two or three. In these cases, guessing is always in your favor even when there is a penalty for guessing.

Also remember to read carefully and *eliminate* the poor options as you go along. Checking off poor choices will allow you to focus on the remaining options and improve your chances that you will discover small differences.

Once an answer has been selected, read the stem one more time to be sure that your selection is actually *an answer to this particular question.* Very often, a student makes a wrong choice due to misreading the question. Wrong options can be selected because the student misread the stem and selected an option that is correct but not the answer to the initial question. On objective tests, 15% of the errors are reading errors. When interviewed about their mistakes, students say, *"Oh, I guess I read that wrong"* 15 percent of the time.

> 15% of
> the errors on
> objective tests
> are reading errors.

Example:
"Geo-synchronous" describes satellites that:
A) are used to relay radio and TV signals from one location back down to a distant location.
B) are accelerated to a very high altitude.
C) are located in orbits that allow them to remain over a specific location on earth.
D) are in orbit over the equator to study the geography of the earth.

In reading this question on a test, the first aspect to notice is that the question actually asks if you know the definition of "Geo-synchronous." This is a very common kind of objective question. It does not ask what advantages, functions, or histories you know concerning the satellites. It only tests to see if you know what "Geo-Synchronous" means.

This careful understanding of the question will help you avoid "A" which is true, but not the answer to the question (a common ploy to catch the student who knows something about satellites but nothing about this course).

"B" is also true but not the answer. It does concern an aspect of these satellites that was given a lot of attention in lecture (a common ploy to catch the student that was not asleep *all the time* in lecture and remembers something about 22,000 miles coming through between naps).

"D" is a ploy to catch the student who has *no clue* about what is going on and anxiously looks for one (a clue, that is). He discovers one in the funny letters "geo" which appear in the question *and* in "D" and he falls for that.

"C" is the correct answer.

For essay tests:

The important guideline here is to answer each question twice—once in outline form and then as an essay answer. If possible, you should write a brief outline on another sheet before beginning each essay answer.

This first answer can be in your own words and shorthand. For example, in response to the question, "What was important about the Gettysburg Address?" you

> The important guideline here is to answer each question twice.

might jot down, *"Lincoln, at graveyard; during Civil War; trying to unite the country; said country must try hard to finish the war; emphasized equality and the people's repre-*

sentation in government; give quote. "

Now, looking at the first answer, you are likely to make the second answer complete and in good form. Also, as you are writing the second answer, new points may come to mind to add to the final answer. The teacher is more likely to give a high score when the major points are easy to find.

The teacher will also find major points more easily if your writing is as neat as possible. If this is a problem, buy several erasable ink pens before your first essay test! Answers written up the side of a crowded page, with scratchouts and little arrows to guide the weary reader, will not get high marks.

Final Exams

If you have a job at college, the most important final exam preparation will be to **ask for a light, or no, schedule during final week.** Do this early because all your fellow workers who are students will ask off for final week when it dawns on them they need it.

Final exams often cover all or most of the material in a course. Most often it is this chance of being asked "nearly anything" that sets off the fear in the hearts of students. Here's the most important place for the make-up-the-test strategy.

If you had a bet with another student about the one question that will be on the test, what would it be? Write down your version of the question. What would be the second most likely question? Write down your version of this question. Continue until you have all your guesses in order.

Now write out the answers. Most students don't *do* this part. They just look up the answers to their own satisfaction. That's not enough practice for this crucial situation. You need practice writing out the answers at least twice— once with your notes and books available and once without.

For final exams in many courses, note cards will be a great way to a good grade. Include old quiz and test questions on the cards along with the ones you made up during the semester from your reading and lectures.

In courses where many individual facts need to be learned, the note cards can be your drill cards. Chemistry, physics, history survey courses, art surveys, and some literature review courses are especially good places for drill cards.

A handful of drill cards can keep you busy and productive in those last hours before an exam when panic has a tendency to set in. Start the cards early in the course so that you're ready!

Final Exams All Come At Once! We all know finals come at one time, but students often only lament the fact and just take the exams in the order they come during final week. Before you take that approach consider this: the value of final exams, the number of credits assigned to the course, and your preparation all vary from course to course.

> Your first final
> may not be
> the most important one
> so you need
> a little smart planning
> of your study time.

For some of your courses, your grade on the final exam may make up half of your grade in the course or more! In other courses, quizzes, tests and other assignments make up most of your grade and the final is only a small part. Your first final may not be the most important one, so you need a little smart planning of your study time. Here's an example:

Final Week

Monday:	2 pm: History Final
Tuesday:	4 pm: Art Appreciation Final
Wednesday:	10 am: Chemistry
	4 pm: English Literature
Thursday:	---- No exams ----
Friday:	2 pm: Psych. Final.
	Paper due in Career Course, no final.

Most of your fellow students will face these challenges as they come. They will study for the History exam until it happens, then switch to Art, panic over having two tests on Wednesday, crash on Thursday, go mad over Psych on Friday afternoon, and go home to wait for the mail that tells them what happened!

There is a better way. Let's assume that the History final counts for about 25% of your final grade (mid-term tests and papers are common in history courses), and let's say the Chemistry final counts for 25% of the grade in that course. Lab reports and other tests make up a large part. For English Lit., the essay final could be half the course grade. And in the Art Appreciation course the final may be a small part of the grade, let's say 10%. Psych may have a 20% final and the Career course has no final at all.

Your grade point average is figured for each credit so that consideration needs to be in your plan.

The "Final Facts" look like this:

History:	Mon. 25% of 3 credits.
	Doing well, I know that stuff.

Art Appr.:   Tues. only 10% of 2 credits
              Need to review notes on the slides.
Chem.:   Wed. 25% of 4 credits
              This is going to be tough!
Eng. Lit.   Wed. 50% of 3 credits
              Need to review authors and dates.
              Thurs. No exams
Psych.:   Fri. 20% of 3 credits
              Multiple choice, like the mid-terms.
Career: Fri. Paper due

It's obvious that reviewing History until Monday after-noon and then spending all day Tuesday on the Art final is going to lead to a bad Tuesday night of panic about Chemistry and English.

A strategy that starts with Chemistry and English where you have the most at stake is best. After keeping up on studying the week before, a good plan would look like this:

Just before final week:
   Saturday:
      Review Chem. notes, make up possible exam questions; drill on all Eng. Lit. cards at least once.
   Sunday:
      Write out answers to possible Chem and Eng. Lit. questions; review all History cards for tomorrow.

Final week:
   Monday:
      Morning: Make up expected History questions and, if time, go back to Chem. or Eng. Lit. cards once today.
      Afternoon: Do History cards to review answers to

possible questions until the exam.

Evening: Review Chemistry, Eng. Lit. cards once, and then spend the rest of the evening on Art notes, especially the ones on the slides.

Tuesday:

Morning: Review Chemistry and Eng. Lit. Cards once.

Afternoon: Review Art notes on slides & lecture & readings until the exam.

Evening: Make up new tests on Chemistry and Eng.Lit courses, try out answers without notes.

Wednesday:

Morning: Chemistry only this morning;

Afternoon: Eng. Lit. cards from 2 to 4.

Evening: Take the night off, sleep late.

Thursday:

Late morning: Make up some new items that might be on the Psych. test; review Psych. notes and old multiple choice exams and quizzes.

Afternoon: Final touches on Career paper, then review reading notes from Psych. textbook.

Friday:

Morning: Review reading notes in Psych once more, review old multiple choice tests and items made up; hand in career paper and confirm ride or plane ticket. **OUT OF HERE!**

This plan for the week puts the focus on the most important exams. The 4-credit Chemistry course has a final worth 25% of the course, a whole credit. And in Eng. Lit., the final counts a credit and a half!

These tests should get your attention from the very first of the week until they are over. The History and Psychology finals have three-fourths of a credit riding on the final and they should get your attention for at least the evening before, and the day of, each test.

Some students who set short-term goals for themselves like this, give themselves rewards as they accomplish each part of their schedule. One of my students had written in her pocket calendar, "Pizza tonight. If History Chapter 7 not reviewed by dinner, plain cheese, no toppings. If it is reviewed, one topping. More than 5 extra study cards on Chapter 7, three toppings!"

Campus Clip: Excuses

One student who missed the final exam in my course explained, *"Sorry I missed your final. I was sick on the chicken."*
"You ate some bad chicken?"
"I didn't eat any. A truck on the Interstate spilled some chicken cages in the traffic. It was disgusting."
Just to keep her from going into details, I gave her the make-up exam—no penalty!

Health During Finals

Many students get sick during finals and it's usually a big disaster. This is not a good time to get sick.

Final week can be the last week of many in which you have abused yourself with little sleep, bad eating, and too much other stuff. The hectic schedule of the semester is likely to have you at a low point already. Final week is not a good time for a change to the worse. Avoid extra stress, if possible. Put off car repairs and big talks about complaints with friends. For example, staying up even later than usual and eating junk food in your room so you can study instead of going to meals, etc., will be dangerous to your whole semester.

> **Many students get sick during finals.**

Cheating

You may feel insulted by this section on academic dishonesty, but remember the pressures to do well and the stress of examinations can distort a person's perspective.

It crosses the mind of every student sometime in college that a little "short-cut" (otherwise known as "cheating") could be done. Most students ignore such temptations. But if you encounter someone thinking of a scheme, remind them of the extra risk in college: your college record, with all its highlights *and blemishes*, will come up again and again throughout your career.

If you cheat at cards or on a golf course, few people will ever know and the consequences for getting caught will be temporary. But college records last longer than any advantage that can be gained by cheating. Any business man will tell you that slight differences in grade-point averages of employees out of college are unimportant. But have a note about cheating on the record and the boss remembers forever.

Cheating on Tests. When panic sets in the last part of the exam hour, a student doing poorly may be tempted. It is never worth it, and the time could be used to give a little extra attention to reading the multiple-choice questions carefully or making a page of an essay answer a little neater. These efforts have a much better chance of improving a student's score *and* they are legal!

Forget the cheating. Use your best study skills and test-taking strategies instead.

Cheating on Assignments. The temptation is sometimes greater to cheat on assignments because you get out of a little work as well as improve your grade, and who's to know how you completed the work?

The extra problem here is that sympathy from faculty, deans, and parents will be less in this "premeditated" crime. Panic cheating in an exam may not be forgiven, but at least it may be understood. Calculated cheating will always

> Your college record, with all its highlights and blemishes, comes up again and again.

bother future potential employers, bank officers, lenders, and government hiring officers.

Cheating on assignments usually involves another person, so the chances of getting caught are high, and they will

---

Campus Clip: Cheating

Two students seemed to be glancing at each other's answer sheets during my final exam. I had used two forms of the sheet, one with the spaces for answers to the multiple choice questions organized across in rows, and the other with the spaces for the answers organized in columns.

In walking around the room, I noticed that both students had almost all the answers wrong and that both were working down the columns although one had evidently missed the fact that his spaces were numbered across.

When they handed in their answer sheets at the same time, I said to the first student, "Oh, I see you had the answer sheet using the rows, and you (looking at his confused and starting-to-panic partner) had the one using the columns. Each made a pathetic little noise and a feeble gesture to retrieve the sheets, but I said it would all work out in the grades. It did.

---

bring you down with them. Just tell them that college will be over soon enough and all you want following you from there is your success!

And instead of the unethical ideas, suggest they try out new study and drill procedures such as computer programs.

How About a Computer Tutor?

How about a computer program to help learning? Computer programs can be helpful, especially if the drills are very similar to the material and assignments of the course.

Math and language programs often have useful drills because the content of the drills and the test questions are almost exactly the same. For programs in other areas where content can vary, you'll need to know *what* history, government, or social studies program would be appropriate.

The famous psychologist B. F. Skinner said computer programs (he called them "teaching machines" in the 1960's) would take over most of the activity in the future schoolrooms of the 1980's and beyond. His prediction was right in that the programs have become an important part of college, but their application is far short of Skinner's expectations. What happened?

> ## Computer learning is far short of Skinner's expectations. What happened?

Skinner felt that success with questions and answers would be enough incentive to keep the student working. But for most of us, the novelty of working the screen wore off long ago and real life applications are needed to keep interest up. Sitting on a chair, even one in front of a computer, may not produce learning that shows up on tests unless you practice the material in a situation and format similar to the test coming up.

A second limitation of computer effectiveness is in the *action* you are asked for. Remember, learning is in the *doing*. If you learn to press the right buttons on a keyboard to answer questions, your performance will be best there and not as good on written tests and new examples.

It's amazing to all of us that learning more math or more names of important people on a computer doesn't result in correct answers on these points on every test after that. You can improve with a computer program, but how the improvement shows up on tests depends on how similar the test is to the program, not only in content, but *in the way you are asked to provide answers.*

Here's another place for "make up some tests." You can construct practice tests on the computer material but in the format and style you know you're going to see on tests later. Quizzes and drills with pencil and paper will give you practice in expressing the answers as required later—when no keyboard is around.

Part III

Keys to Avoiding
the 4 Big Mistakes

Chapter 8

The 4 Big Mistakes
in Habits, Housing, Health Care,
and Management of Time and Money

Your move to college has some danger points. Choices you haven't worried about up to now are suddenly crucial. College can be so hectic that the importance of daily choices can be missed. For example, what to do with the time between classes and after dinner may seem trivial, but experienced students often list time management as one of the hardest parts of college. Bad habits that creep into your routine and poor decisions about housing and health care all can have effects that will last all through college.

Mistake Number 1: Habits
"Great! I'm Free To Develop My Own Bad Habits!"

Your habits are bound to change when you go to a new place with new people and new freedom. You can do what you want to do! Many new students, free of high school and parents, look forward to that! No more critics looking at everything you do. Well, at least a clean slate with a new set of critics. Your usual caretakers are not around anymore.

It's a good time to try being a little different, but it's also a good time to look out for yourself! The most dangerous habits are (1) the substances you take; (2) the routines that wear you down; and (3) a poor diet.

> **Your usual caretakers are not around anymore.**

Example #1—The Substances You Take.

Alcohol, drugs and medications are easy to lose track of in the rush of college life. The student's most common mistake in this area is with drinking habits. The alcohol habit is a contagious pitfall because many feel "loosened up" socially, get a high, or temporarily escape from their problems.

Beyond the usual problems you've heard so many times, remember that alcohol is a depressant, and since depression is most common in college students, you don't need anything that adds to that! So take care, you will know many students who will ruin their college careers with too much drinking.

> **Alcohol is a depressant, and since depression is most common in college students, you don't need anything that adds to that!**

There's an extra danger here for women. Fifty percent of women sexually assaulted on campus have been drinking at the time—making themselves more vulnerable—at least in the eye of the one doing the assaulting.

The majority of mothers with unwanted pregnancies in

the college-age group report they had been drinking at the time of the "mistake."

Illegal drugs may get the most attention but the *number* of college students ignorant enough to be made miserable by drugs is much lower than the number of students abusing alcohol. Although the *extent* of the misery may be worse with drugs, all of us are at risk of addiction to alcohol and its deteriorating effects on the liver, stomach, and brain (not to mention the mind).

Example #2—The Balance in Your Daily Routines.

Any of us can be addicted to work, entertainment, computers, or partying at least as easily as we can be addicted to alcohol. Skipping sleep, meals, or exercise in order to study, work, or party, will make getting sick more likely.

> Skipping sleep, food, or exercise in order to study, work, or party, will make getting sick more likely.

When you start feeling bad, review your usual daily habits—you can often find the answer there.

The common mistake is in pursuing "a good time" or a work schedule that is just too heavy ("I gotta get this stuff done, so I can get some more stuff going!")

Consider the adults you have known while growing up, does any of this sound familiar?

Example #3—The Stuff You Eat Everyday.

It's easy to "overdose" on salt, fat, sugar, and caffeine. This can make you sleep poorly, therefore need *more* sleep, feel tired and then depressed. Students who "sleep in" too often, usually can trace their problem to these intakes.

Depression is a danger in college life because of fatigue, guilt about studies, loneliness, or disappointment in college, where freedom was expected to make life more fun but the four mistakes have interfered.

Check your diet and exercise. Usually a physical activity helps depression, while sugar, alcohol, and over-eating worsen it. To alleviate the guilt factor, try some of the note cards and study habits of Part II.

Mistake Number 2: Housing
"Let's Get a Place Away from Campus;
It Won't Cost as Much!"

Students often consider only rent when comparing off-campus and on-campus housing. Dorms may seem expensive when you consider that you only get one room and most of the time only half of that. Other dorms may have shared study rooms or living rooms but a private kitchen is rare and rules about food, quiet hours, and drinking can seem juvenile.

Before you conclude that the best idea is to live off campus, you need to investigate a little more because off-campus living has inconveniences too. Shopping for, and preparing, your own meals, the time lost in commuting from your off-campus home, and the expense of it all come to mind first, but the survey coming up in Chapter 9 shows that off-campus living leaves you feeling disconnected from what's going on at the school.

> The survey coming up shows that off-campus living leaves you feeling disconnected.

Students who feel a little disconnected are more likely

to drop out—becoming totally disconnected—from college. Living off-campus often just makes it harder to hang around for other activities or to get back to campus for social events, interest groups, cooperative studying, and socializing. Living off-campus may also tempt you to put in more hours at an outside job since you are off-campus anyway.

Whatever the reason, you'll see that the survey shows that commuters are at a greater risk of drifting away from, and then dropping out of college.

Mistake Number 3: Health Care
"I'm Young, I'm Healthy, What's the Problem??"

With no parents around to furnish corrections and reminders, many students develop their own style of taking care of themselves and that's, hopefully, a good part of going off to college. As you look around at college, you will see students who are taking care of themselves just fine, and you will see some real failures.

You would think that the most attention would be given to taking care of number one, but self-abuse is a common condition—and college students are no exception.

The general health of college students is not good. Whether it's because the feeling of independence leads to laziness about diet and exercise, or just an inclination to party too much, students do get sick often. Illness leads to missing classes, less studying, less fun, and more time away from school. Watch what you're

> You will see students who are taking care of themselves just fine, and you will see some real failures.

doing to yourself; it could make college less fun and take you closer to dropping out.

Now is the time for you to start remembering for yourself such things as 6-month dental check-ups, routine physicals, protective innoculations (when was your last flu or tetanus shot?), not to mention the obvious ones of eating balanced meals, washing your clothes, etc., etc.

Make sure you know all you need to know about your medical records. Do you have prescriptions for any medicines you take on a regular basis? If you have a chronic condition, is there a specialist near the college to turn to, if necessary? Do you have complete information on any allergies to medications that a physician might need to know in treating you in an emergency?

Also, as mentioned earlier, depression and anxiety are common among college students. If you find yourself easily upset, crying for little cause, or feeling unusually anxious or depressed, take advantage of the free counseling services usually available at most campuses.

You are probably very aware of the consequences of unprotected sex—AIDS and genital herpes won't go away. Here again, alcohol and drug abuse play a major part in unprotected sex.

Your campus will have health care and counseling facilities for students. Use their services.

Mistake Number 4: Management
"I Need to Drop a Couple of Courses, and Buy Some More CD's"

Time Management.

At your first registration I suggested that you keep the number of courses you take at the average or a little below. It takes a semester to learn how to manage your time for handling course work. Hopefully, a typical week's chart such as the one on page 63 will help. But a habit of signing up for the minimum or dropping courses when things get tough, can waste too much time and you may complain: *"I've been here a whole year and I've only got 18 credits! This whole thing is a waste of time and money."*

Dangerous decisions that can get you into this problem are:

1. Holding back on registering for courses in order to make too much time for work;
2. Dropping classes because you don't want to get up early;
3. Cutting a class until it's too embarrassing to go back, so you drop instead.

Don't trap *yourself* into feeling you are not making enough progress.

Money Management.

The same feeling of frustration can develop from mismanaging money just as it can from mismanaging time.

> "I've been here a whole year and I've only got 18 credits."

If you always feel you are out of money, don't have enough, or waste too much, you eventually will come up with the idea of taking on more hours at a job at the cost of study time and other campus activities, or you may be tempted by the idea of dropping out for awhile—just to earn more money.

Keep close track of the money and the credit card. Many businesses will constantly offer you more credit cards and more opportunities to buy new things. The last thing you need is more demands to make you feel depressed! Keep your financial life as simple as possible.

Resist All Vultures.

Often there is more than money at stake when the vultures target a student. Groups advocating everything from just another philosophy to violence and criminal activities are active on every campus. Spend your time as carefully as you spend your money and don't risk a commitment to a group that might result in an entry in your college file or a police record.

Keep Your Records Up to Date

Your time and money in college build a record in the college offices of your courses, credits, grades, and progress. When you make any change in your program, be sure your record is updated. For example, if you decide not to continue a course, a formal drop of the course is important. Otherwise the instructor may just fail you for not showing up.

I asked one student how her biology course was going, and she said,

"It didn't work out. I got so far behind in lab, I was embarrassed to go. I'll try again next semester when

I have a better schedule. "

"You dropped it?"

"I just didn't go back anymore. They'll figure it out, won't they?"

"They're likely to give you an 'F'. "

"What! I can't have an 'F.'"

Update your record.

Chapter 9
The 4 Big Mistakes and Who Graduates, Who Doesn't

You need the very best grades you can accomplish—for your record, your future résumé, and to get into special courses and programs in the later years of college. Many majors require grade-point levels higher than the average.

But grades are seldom the problem that leads to dropping out. Low grades can be discouraging and may be a part of a student's final decision to drop out, but other factors begin affecting that decision earlier.

Living conditions, working long hours at an outside job, and commuting a long way to school, are all factors tending to separate a student from school.

> Grades are seldom the problem that leads to dropping out.

These factors may eventually result in low grades, but the determination of who graduates and who doesn't starts long before the grades are passed out. Even students who have good grades sometimes quit because of these "separation factors." When grades are a factor in dropping out, they come as a clincher after a long bout with other mistakes!

The Student Success Survey

At the University of Maryland, 910 students were given a survey about their college situation. Of these students, 455 had decided to drop out and filled out the survey while waiting in the Records Office to do the last of the paper work. The other 455 students filled out the survey in their Psychology class—none from this second half were in the process of dropping out.

Read the survey (see the Appendix) for a little more understanding of factors in college life that are not covered in newspapers and books. Notice that although the survey concerns college *success*, many questions are about *college life* in general and not directly related to *college performance*. The students' living conditions, social situations, jobs, and commuting times all influenced their spirit for college and their progress in it.

> Even students who have good grades sometimes quit because of these "separation factors."

The items were changed in some cases for students in the psychology class. Since they were not dropping out, that assumption was taken out along with the use of the past tense. For example, for the Psych students Item 1 said, "Where are you living ..." and Item 16 said, "If a student decided to leave UM, the following could be factors in a student's decision. If you were to leave, what reasons do you think would apply to your situation?"

Survey Results

Comparisons of the answers from students dropping out with those of students not dropping out showed important differences. They are presented in the table on page 109.

Grades:

Grades between terminating and ongoing students were nearly the same and averaged well within the acceptable range. Terminating students did have a slightly lower grade average but by the standards of the college, almost all were still doing a satisfactory job!

Housing:

One of the nine most important differences presented in the table on page 109 is living arrangements.

Of the terminating students, 85% lived off campus while only 39% of on-

> Of the terminating students, 85% lived off campus while only 39% of on-going students lived off campus.

going students lived off campus. So living on campus isn't necessarily the crucial factor to staying in college (39% of the on-going students seem to be managing while living off campus), but living off campus is more likely to be a habit of the terminating student.

Commuting:

The next item has to do with how far the student lives from campus, or how far the student has to go to classes whether he or she lives on campus or not. Terminating students needed 19 minutes; ongoing students, 6 minutes.

Jobs:

The next three items ask about how the student is handling the "outside job" problem. Of the terminating students, 70% worked off-campus, averaged 22 minutes work-commuting time, and averaged more than 20 hours a week at a job. Of on-going students, only 29% worked off campus; they averaged about 9 minutes work-commuting time, and averaged 5 hours a week at the job.

The last of the nine most important questions had to do with expenses, plans for the future, and time for socializing and friends.

Factors That <u>Didn't</u> Relate to Dropping Out

It's interesting to note which questions did *not* produce different answers from drop-outs and successful students. We already know that only a few students drop out because of unacceptable (to the college) grades. But also the lack of selecting a major did not relate to dropping out. Successful students seem to be doing just fine without an early decision on this point, and many drop-outs said they had declared a major, but were leaving anyway.

And no reason from the long list of possible dissatisfactions was selected more often by one group than by the other.

Risk Factors That Added Up to Dropping Out

So living arrangements, commuting time to school and work, work hours, expenses, plans for the future, free time, and availability of friends *all* play important roles in influencing a person's spirit for college.

Many students—both drop-outs and successful ones—

had more than one of the nine "separation factors." Actually, almost all students in both groups had one or more separation factors. For example, a student living off campus often had a long commute to classes as well, and possibly a long work commute, and few friends on campus, and long hours on the job.

As the factors build up for an individual, the chances of success in college go down. When we gave each student a score from 0 to 9 according to how many separation factors he or she had, you can see in the graph on page 108 that successful students generally had low scores. For example, almost all of the students with just two risk (of dropping out) factors were students in the on-going, successful group. But almost all of the students with seven risk factors were drop-outs. Students with more than six risk factors had little chance of being successful.

> As the number of "wrong things" builds up, the chances that the student will finish college become almost zero!

Now a word of caution about jumping to conclusions. You can see that for each risk level, some on-going students were doing many of "the wrong things" and still getting along. But the odds were building against them.

> The lack of selecting a major did not relate to dropping out.

Of course, you can see a few drop-out cases where the student was making very few mistakes but was a drop-out nevertheless. However, the generalization holds up that as the number of "wrong things" builds up, the chances that the student will finish college become almost zero!

Risk Factor Survey Results

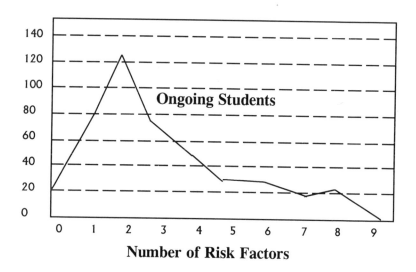

Ongoing Students

Number of Risk Factors

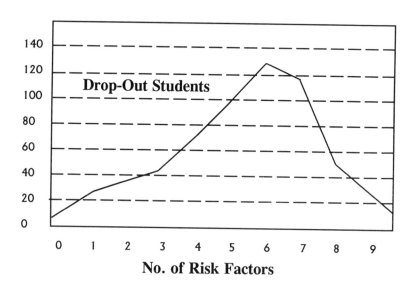

Drop-Out Students

No. of Risk Factors

Students Who Drop Out Part of the Way
Are Likely to Drop Out All the Way

Item in order of importance	Students Dropping Out	On-going Students
1. Living Arrangements	85% live off-campus	39% live off-campus
2. Time Spent Commuting to College (average no. of minutes)	18.7 minutes	6.2 minutes
3. No. Who Work Off-Campus	70%	29%
4. Time Spent Commuting to Work	21.8 minutes	8.7 minutes
5. Hours/Week Working	20.5 hours	5 hours
6. Percent of Expenses Provided by Student	50.3%	15.4%
7. Plans Upon (If) Leaving	49% plan to continue education	58% plan to continue education
8. Time Spent Socializing On Campus	62% no extra time	37% no extra time
9. No. of Friends on Campus	64% had 2 or less	31% had 2 or less

Changing Colleges

Changing colleges is one way to get a new start with reduced risk factors and could be a reasonable solution to the expenses of college. For example, many students start at a community college, saving money and getting required courses out of the way. Later, they switch to the larger school to complete the major they select.

This strategy has risks because some courses, when transferred to the second school, may not be accepted as fulfilling requirements as intended. The strategy requires contacting an academic advisor at the second school and confirming that the particular courses you take will count in the future program the way you plan.

Be prepared for the shock that a few credits might not count. You could make up for this by taking a heavier course load in another semester along the way, or just not graduating in the year you first intended. "On time" is only in the eye of the beholder.

It may occur to you along the way that if you're not happy here, you might be happy somewhere else. But changing colleges for social reasons is a risky prospect. Why would the next place be better when it didn't seem so when you made your first choice?

Two transfer students ask an unusually wise senior:

First TS: *"Are the people friendly on this campus?"*

Senior: *"How were they at your old school?"*

First TS: *"Really clickish. If you weren't part of the 'in' crowd, they never asked you to do anything."*

Senior: *"That's how you'll find them here."*

Second TS: *"At my old school, the people were pretty friendly if you made an effort."*

Senior: *"That's how you'll find them here."*

First TS: *"Hey, how can they be clickish and friendly?"*

Senior: *"You only find what you look for."*

A little soul-searching is in order here. Perhaps changing a few activities, clubs, sports, or friends right where you are would take care of the problem. No sense chasing after the perfect place when there isn't one.

When the decision turns out to be in favor of changing colleges in spite of the soul-searching, the best advice is to be sure to check a number of things at the new school *before* transferring—several semesters before, if possible. Many times I have heard from a transfer student, *"I thought all my credits from CC would count. The math I suffered through at CC is not enough??? I have to take another math!?!"*

Here's what you need to check:

1. Will all your credits transfer?
2. How will the courses you've already taken "count?" That is, are they acceptable for fulfilling requirements at the second school?
3. How are the courses in your major set up? When are they offered? Often because of required sequences, you will not be able to take all the courses you need in the few semesters you have left.
4. Check living accommodations.
5. Check all those things that concerned you the first time.
6. Review your College Questions and Answers from Part I.

Your Campus Social Life

Roommates. For freshmen, roommates are often picked at random or by a computer. Many colleges use a questionnaire to match roommates. In later semesters students switch around making their own choices. So if you have the chance, what questions should you ask a roommate?

> What questions should you ask a roommate?

The crucial aspects of roommates are similar to the crucial aspects of the four big mistakes. Habits of smoking, drinking, eating, and housing preference need to be considered, of course, but also attitudes on health, money management, and time spent partying. You might also ask about habits concerning neatness and attitudes about visitors—especially boyfriend-girlfriend visitors! All of these will influence how two roommates get along.

Significant Others, Choosing Friends.

This topic relates to staying in college because a troublesome relationship can use up a lot of time, effort, and spirit.

In counseling students about romantic problems, I notice that the same questions come up almost every time. So without getting into a long discussion of the nature of true love, the dangers of irresponsible sex, and the pros and cons of getting "serious," I have listed some questions that might help you keep a comfortable perspective on a college romance.

Unfortunately, you will have to provide most of the answers about your own particular situation.

Questions About Friends

Question #1: Can your friends play fair?

When the first irritation in a relationship pops up, it's likely to be about a fair balance between selfish considerations and a consideration for the other person. Friends, studies, work, and classes demand so much of a college schedule that inconsiderate and unfair demands from a boy or girl friend can signal a problem very quickly.

The first step toward resolving the unfair demands problem is an understanding that a need for time for other activities shouldn't be taken as personal rejection. Some boy or girl friends feel that *any* time given to other demands means you think less of them. If the relationship is to last even through final week, this must be discussed (see Question 2).

A second step toward resolving unfair demands is in the answer to this, "I can get interested in your interests (your friends, your sports, your studies); can you get interested in mine?" Everyone has an obsession (sport, habit, music, lifestyle) that they want you to buy into, but is it fair to insist that only their's are important?

> Everyone has an obsession (sport, habit, music, lifestyle) that they want you to buy into.

A great deal of the conflict about unfair demands has to do with how you spend your time—together, apart, and with other people and other projects. You can make time for someone, but you have to take it from somewhere! So here's Question #2: Can we talk?

Question #2: Can we talk? Can *you* listen? Can *I* listen?

Talking and listening take up a lot of everyone's time.

Most people seem to have the talking part down pretty well but may come up short on listening skills.

If we meet someday and you tell me you used only one idea in this part about relationships, I hope it's this part on listening skills.

First, we all neglect the physical part of listening now and then. Everyone needs a reminder to look at the person who is talking. It's nerve-wracking to have a person stare at you while you're talking, but a person who constantly looks somewhere else also frustrates his/her conversational partner.

In order to look at someone, you have to face him or her. It can be casual; there's no need to be "in their face" through the whole talk, but we all know that uncomfortable feeling when someone becomes distracted or actually walks away while we struggle to keep up and finish what we want to say. So **face up** to your listening responsibility!

> A person who always looks somewhere else frustrates his/her conversational partner.

A second part of listening is to be aware of other aspects of posture that may send the wrong messages. Slumping, stretching, and fidgeting all indicate a lack of attention.

In addition to the physical part of listening, there are some handy conversation rules:

Conversation Rule #1: Avoid too many "you" statements that appear critical. Many people are most interested in themselves. They tune in to the parts of conversation that are about them, and they are less interested in the rest. The most important part of the conversation will be, "What does the message say about *me*?" So they will resent remarks that seem to blame them for mistakes or criticize their point of view even in the most subtle way:

> *"So you just slept in and cut class for no reason?"*
> *"Hey, I had a reason, I was tired!"*
> *"Have you done any planning for the Thursday night party?"*
> *"I can't do everything at once, I'll get to it when this test is over, OK?"*

If you can avoid the judgments implied in these questions by phrasing them in an impersonal way rather than using "you," the answer may be less argumentative:

> *"So I thought class was kind of interesting today."*
> *"I was so tired, I just slept in."*
> *"This Thursday night party is going to be big."*
> *"As soon as I get this test over, I'll work on it."*

These kinds of conversations may not always work out this well, but you have a better chance when the implication of blame is kept out of them.

One habit that helps avoid the pitfall of appearing too critical of the other person is to put topics on an impersonal basis, using "it" instead of "you." When a conversation seems threatening, try to look at the problem as an "it" instead of "you" or "me."

For example, saying *"You didn't remember to pick up the books!"* immediately puts the other person on the defensive. Saying instead, *"It's going to be hard to study without the books we need"* opens the way for the other person to make amends, perhaps by going back for the books!

This tactic avoids the trap of "attack, defense, and counter-attack." You can defuse arguments and confrontations by showing interest in the other person's experiences, without focusing on personal blame or emphasizing mistakes.

Conversation Rule #2: Avoid suggesting solutions too soon. People are often tempted to suggest solutions to problems: *"Why don't you . . ."* *"You should try..."* *"Don't be so . . ."* They mean well but they often strike the listener as being pushy and superior. Most of us don't react kindly to suggestions and quick solutions.

If you told me you're frequently late for work because of traffic, and I said you should go another way, you would be offended.

> You: *The traffic really made me late today!*
>
> Me: *Why didn't you turn off of Main Street.*
>
> You: *That wouldn't help.* (We are in an argument already!)
>
> Me: *Yes it would. You should try those side streets.*
>
> You: *That's out of the way.*
>
> Me: *Don't be so rigid! Try out those other ways.*
>
> You: *Why don't you mind your own business!*
>
> Me: *Hey, you brought up the problem, not me. I was just trying...*

Yes, I was just trying to give quick advice, but you feel I was being critical. Efficiency in conversation is for business meetings and TV shows where time is short. Friendly conversation should be enjoyed; people who *just* want to fix things often offend others who interpret their attempt at helpfulness as "acting superior."

Conversation Rule #3: Send a friendly message; avoid the put-downs. The habit of being a critic can develop slowly so a friend may be unaware of his or her new style. Friendship can sour when one friend expands occasional friendly advice to frequent put-downs and sarcasm. Everyone has plenty of critics and would like to avoid new ones.

As one student about to break up with her boyfriend said, "I thought his 'attitude' was kind of clever until he started using it on me!"

Friends are for liking. Be sure you send the right message often and watch out for "friends" who don't.

These conversation rules can help you with Question #3.

Question #3: Are we handling problems or just playing games? A talk about problems will take more than a listening effort on both sides. It takes an effort to find the good things another person is doing. If all you hear is what you are doing wrong, then, in the long run, you feel the person doesn't like you and it's down hill from there.

Problems are seldom solved by critics because they focus on blame instead of answers. How does your boy or girl friend measure up on this critic vs. friend dimension?

> Problems are seldom solved by critics because they focus on blame instead of answers.

Friends bring out the best in me. When we meet, their attention sweeps the common ground between us looking for sparkles to highlight. I like the "me" they draw out. I return the compliment, like a friendly searchlight, seeking the best in them.

Some people have another focus. Their search overlooks the good in us and zeros in on vulnerable spots. We pull back and risk very little because we know what they're looking for. We cover up.

Aim *your* searchlight carefully. What are you looking for?

Here are a few of the "games" that go on when "friends" are only serving their own interests.

GAME 1: "Do as I say and I won't get mad."

When talking to students about romance problems, I sometimes ask about the everyday events:

"Does he come on time?"

"Sometimes."

"Are you always ready?"

"Yes."

"Do you go where he wants to go or where you want to go?"

"We do his thing."

"Do you talk about his topics or yours?"

"Mostly his."

"Sounds a little one-sided?"

"Yes."

"What would happen if you were not ready?"

"He would be mad."

"What if you went to your thing?"

"He would get mad and pout."

"What if you went on about your topic?"

"He would get mad."

This is a common situation where one person accommodates the other out of fear, *"He/she will get mad!"* In a way, both get rewarded. One person gets his/her way, and the other avoids a big blow-up.

> It's a classic relationship where one gets the positive and the other avoids the negative.

That's the reward that keeps half the couple trying to please. This is a classic relationship where one gets the positive and the other avoids the negative.

GAME 2: "I'll bet you can't make me happy."

This game involves a complainer who is never satisfied. She (could be a 'he') always has a problem, and others are always scrambling around trying to fix it. So our complainer gets attention and keeps the game going by never admitting the fix is good enough.

GAME 3: "My problem is your problem."

In this game the complainer hooks others into temporarily working out the problem. Life is easier if others take your responsibilities. The ultimate version of this game is "My Problem is: You Won't Change." Again it is a means for shifting the responsibility to the partner.

> *"I have to have this report and these botany samples in by Friday! Do you have any more of those plastic pockets for samples?"*
>
> *"I only have two."*
>
> *"Two? I need about 20. Could you go down to the store for some more?"*
>
> *"What? No I can't. I have to review my note cards for Physics."*
>
> *"You'll need some more for your next report anyway."*
>
> *"I don't have a car."*
>
> *"You could borrow Jim's. That would fix your problem."*
>
> *"My problem?"*

You can see where this is going. The next example is a little more personal because it demands that another person take on the problem *and* change:

> *"You're always late."*
> *"I have lots of things to do in the afternnon."*
> *"Well, it makes us late for dinner."*
> *"Why don't you go on your own?"*
> *"I'll wait, but you have to start getting here earlier!"*

This puts on the pressure and the guilt. If this kind of conversation becomes the habit, someone is going to want out of this relationship.

GAME 4: "It's not my fault; you made me do it."

> *"Why do you get mad so much?"*
> *"Well, I wouldn't if you didn't always..."*

> *"Why do you drink so much?"*
> *"Because you don't pay enough attention to me."*

Beware of excuses that target "you"—the shift in blame is coming your way.

> *"That junk food is not good for you."*
> *"I haven't got time to go down to the caf."*
> *"You should, though, that's just salt, fat, and sugar."*
> *"I would go to the cafeteria more, but you never come and get me when you go down to dinner."*
> *"Well, I'll try harder. Hey, wait a minute, your junk food habit is your problem!"*

GAME 5: "If you really loved me...."

You might think the If-you-really-loved-me argument would only come up in arguments about sex, but it's often used as a lever after "I'll bet you can't make me happy" has failed to produce the desired result.

After a series of complaints, responded to with a suggestion of what might help, the complainer might be met with, *"Well, I guess you will have to help yourself!"* That ought to stop some of the complaining in "I'll-bet-you-can't-make-me-happy."

But in this new Game 5, the complainer responds again with, *"Well, if you really loved me, you would come up with an answer to my problem."* If successful, this game can be a good solution for the complainer because it ends with, *"My problem is (now) your problem."*

> You might think the If-you-really-loved-me argument would only come up in arguments about sex.

Games are most often attempts to blame a lover or friend for current problems. If these ploys result in all the blame and responsibility going to you, it's not a fair relationship.

Question #4: Is this relationship about liking as well as loving? Loving is a message sent on rare occasions. The message of whether we like a person or don't like them is sent everyday in several ways: by the listening style used, the conversation habits, the games that are played, and whose problems are taken seriously.

> The relationship is unfair if the message is, "I love you, I just don't like you."

Sometimes a partner won't listen, won't play fair with responsibilities and problems, and becomes your constant critic. In these cases, claims of love can't make up for the message of criticism. Again the relationship is unfair if the message is, "I love you, I just don't *like* you."

So there you have the four big mistakes. When things seem to be going wrong, take a break and look over your situation—your habits, your housing, your health care, and how you are spending time and money.

The college years can be an exciting adventure in your life as well as preparation for a productive and enjoyable career.

Your future happiness will mostly be up to you. Take responsibility for it, and don't give that responsibility to anyone else. No one else has quite the same interest in your happiness as you do.

The college adventure will enhance your future happiness by teaching you how to learn and how to care for yourself and your social life. This will always be an advantage. College offers you a valuable gift in career, income potential and quality of life. Have a great adventure!

During your college adventure, check in at home now and then. Read Part IV just to learn a little more about your parents' perspective. Then pass the book along to them so that everyone has a realistic view of what's coming up.

PART IV

What Can An Anxious Parent Do?

Chapter 10
Helping Your College-Bound Student Take Flight

Is This Trip Necessary?

Parents are bound to have many anxieties about their college freshman son or daughter. Trips to visit college campuses can be an early opportunity to manage your uneasiness. Travel costs for these fact-finding missions are small expenses when compared to your investment in four years of college and the effect of those years on all the years to come. Be as liberal as possible in decisions to visit colleges.

As the field of choices narrows, a second visit to campuses already investigated may also be money well spent. The questions will have changed, and your son or daughter will be more informed about the important issues of college.

Usually you will have visited the most likely school early when the priority of questions and interests were still forming. Near the end of the selection process, the most likely school will probably still be near the top but the memory for details may have faded. A second trip to that original favorite is definitely in order now that comparisons are possible. Your son or daughter can be a more sophisticated visitor.

Helping with the Final Decision

Beyond setting limits on what is financially possible, your interest, advice, and experience are still valuable here. Many parents back out too soon with, *"It's your decision!"*

In most families, parents can contribute much more with their extra assertiveness when it comes to calling, one more time, to ask about details. Does college X really offer internships in psychology? Do you have to be an upperclassman to qualify? Will your would-be college student call to find out? This is not a good time to "have her learn how to do such things" if that means she will rationalize not doing it.

> Your interest, advice, and experience are still valuable here.

You can also help by making up a comparison table of your own. It could be a lot less detailed version of the one on pages 30-31.

Comparing your table with his or hers may uncover differences and reservations that have been unspoken until now.

Once the decision is made, get excited about it. Even if your budding college student thinks getting excited is "uncool." An important decision has been made and your son's or daughter's enthusiasm needs to be supported—as hidden as it may be.

Encourage Your Pride and Joy Carefully

Some parents are tempted to take great pride in how long and hard their college student works and the hardships they endure. It is gratifying to see him or her taking advantage of the opportunities, but it is possible to encourage too much: *"Jane is wonderful. She's carrying 19 credits, works 30 hours a week, reads to the blind on Saturdays, sings in the church choir, and is up till two every night!"*

Many whirlwinds such as Jane burn out early and are dead calm before the year is out—sick, tired, cynical and only 18 years old! Kids with all that energy don't need extra encouragement to abuse themselves. Be sensitive and satisfied with the pace of your off-spring-now-sprung without encouraging a maddening schedule. Note the statistics in Chapter 9.

The "Off-to-College" Shower

How about an "Off-To-College" shower? An evening send-off with all the friends and relatives invited.

Each guest might bring a small gift, the result of their thought on, *"When I was in college, I had a little... (travel kit organizer for toiletries, a pack of erasable-ink pens, or a phone card). It was the best help."* My sister-in-law gave my daughter a $10 roll of quarters for the laundry—not a four-year supply, but a very thoughtful gift.

The gifts are not the important part. It's the feeling of support from the larger family expressing good luck.

A helpful detail to add to the "Off-To-College" shower is a request that each guest write a little "tip" on their greeting card or perhaps in a guest book. *"When I was in col-*

lege, the best thing I did was ... join the chess club ...take up dancing... run every morning... have a good breakfast every morning. "

Campus Clip: **Prepare Your Student Well**

One student thinking of quitting complained to me that the big, impersonal university provided no help with the little things.

> *"I just can't handle it. You should see my room. One corner is piled with dirty laundry; you wouldn't want to put your hand to the bottom of it. "*
> *"The dorm has a laundry, doesn't it?"*
> *"Yes, but I don't know about all those cycles and what goes with what. Once I tried it and all my underwear came out pink!"*
> *"How about buying all new stuff, "* I joked. *"Just throw out the old stuff. "*
> Taking me seriously, he started to cry.
> *"What's wrong?"*
> *"I can't do that. "*
> *"Throw out the old stuff?"*
> *"No, shop for the new stuff. "*
> *"Why not?"*
> *"I don't know my size!"*

He was 19 and still dependent. Mom and Dad did the shopping and had never pointed out the little numbers following him around on his underwear!

Worries

Safety, drugs, alcohol, and sex. The possibilities just drive you crazy! How are parents to help, now that their student is way over there?

I wish I had a fool-proof answer for you on this one, you know I don't. One question about these anxieties is to consider why *you* don't abuse these danger areas. The first reaction of most parents is, *"Well, I know what the consequences are; some of these kids just don't seem to care!"*

Usually the kids do have knowledge of the consequences and that is going to be a help. Also, they need the pride in themselves to resist these dangerous behaviors. Many young drug abusers I have counseled have said, *"What have I got to lose??"* And we parents are flabbergasted! What have you got to lose!?! You have your whole life ahead of you...etc. etc.

You and I are not going to get into any pills or little white powders today, I assume. And it's not likely we will have a drink at lunch either. Why not? Partly because we think too much of ourselves! I have this writing to continue this afternoon. You have your job and important activities to do. We think it is important, we value our work, and we are not about to give it away by being stupid.

Now is the time to give your student the same pride. Express your respect for what your college-student-to-be is doing. How important, interesting and worthwhile it all is! **This is not the time for,** *"Now remember how much trouble you had in high school; you just have to try to keep up with those bright college kids!"* Nor is it time for, *"Some of those college courses are useless in the real world; you just have to stick with it to get that degree."*

Do not belittle the task, that only belittles the person doing the task. It makes them vulnerable to, *"What have I got to lose? I'm not doing anything really important anyway!"*

> Do not belittle the task; that only belittles the person doing the task.

This *is* **a good time for**, *"What a great chance you have. With your common sense and good insights into what's really important, you're going to get a lot out of college!"* and *"You'll be one of the best."*

Worries and Modeling

As much as your sons and daughters may insist they are different from you, they do a lot of imitating. When we look back on our own lives, aren't we amazed how similar we are to our parents?

Worried about your soon-to-be-college-student's drinking habits. What example do *you* set?

Feelings of Loss

All parents feel that the growing up is a little too fast. Part of our purpose in life has been raising this child and now she/he's going away. It's natural to feel a little left behind or a little empty. Help can come from staying interested in the details of their college experience.

Join the parents' association right away! You need to be kept informed about: college activities, how others are handling their changing parental role and learning to let go, and how others are handling their value of themselves now that the student is gone. You need some company in that feeling of, *"I'm only a checkbook"* and *"I'm the only parent having trouble adjusting to this."*

Avoid laying this depression on your soon-to-be-on-his-own student. It can produce an unusual kind of guilt that can erode the spirit for college work.

"Your little sister really misses you, and I can barely get things done around here without you." This was the end of the last letter one parent I know sent her daughter at college and I quote with her permission. It was the last letter because right after that her daughter quit college and came home to work in their restaurant.

Of course, she quit for many reasons found in the statistics in Chapter 9 of this book. I don't blame the mother or her letter as principal causes. But it added to the emotional burden of one who already was having trouble in college.

Feelings of loss of companionship and one of your main projects in life has to be muted for awhile. A parent's duty here is to encourage the student forward, not back.

Campus Clip: **Parent Attitudes**

Some parents miss their teen-now-growing-up; some have another attitude.

Talking on the phone to a father whose son had flunked every course in his first semester, I said, *"I'm sure it's a disappointment to you after helping with applications and all, and then, of course, the wasted money."*

"Well, it was a lot of trouble, but the money wasn't wasted."

"But the whole semester is gone, and he has no credits."

"Yes, but he's not here, he's down there, isn't he?

What Parents Need to Know

Keeping up to date on college is important. You can help if you know what's going on. Guard against losing interest. Ask about progress, credits, and requirements, and learn what they mean in your student's case.

We have a summer orientation for new students, as most schools do. For first-time freshmen, I provided a program for the 300 or so parents that came to the campus with their new students. We explained the program, gave tours, and answered questions—don't miss yours.

We also have a similar program for new transfer students coming from community, and other, colleges—about the same number of transfer students as freshmen. No parent program was necessary for this second group. Only one or two parents usually showed up, and I would take them on a special tour, discuss programs, and answer questions.

Where were all the rest of the parents of the transfer students? Having gone once before at the other school, they felt they knew enough, or their interest had just waned.

Keep informed, stay close.

Many counselors have found that the high-risk students do well when they have supportive parents who remain flexible and approving as their student tries out changes in jobs, schedules, and majors.

For further reading on the topic of how parents can help, see Peterson's (of Princeton, NJ) *Smart Parents Guide to College* by Ernest L. Boyer, 1996. Peterson's also has a website: **http//www.petersons.com**

Why Go to College?

College is in the business of helping people learn, grow, and change. The college experience is an intermediate step between parental protection and the cold world where the people around your son or daughter may think they are through with learning and through with looking ahead.

Students often believe that if only they could get through college, the demands of learning and tests would be over. But after graduation, they learn that new learning tasks are always presenting themselves both on the job and at home.

Many of the specifics of their classes will be forgotten, but the means for finding and learning them again will prepare your student for most challenges. Students with good learning skills will always have an easier and more enjoyable experience with changing job and career requirements.

College will also enhance the life you have planned and anticipate for your son or daughter. It can provide an appreciation of literature, music, and scientific discovery that may only be possible through a college experience.

And, of course, your son or daughter should go to college because of what they will gain in earnings. A college education will increase potential life earnings by $500,000 on the average (1997 dollars). And your student will have a better understanding of what money cannot do as well as the good it can accomplish.

So it is a precious gift you are giving, both in income potential and quality of life. Nurture your investment, check on it as you would any other. You deserve a big thank you not only from your son or daughter but from all of us who will benefit from the talents and competencies that he or she will develop.

APPENDICES

RESOURCES

Most of these resources are revised each year. Be sure to use the latest edition of each guide you select.

COLLEGE SELECTION

The Best College for You published by The Princeton Review (not related to Princeton University) and Time Inc. in a magazine format The book lists costs, admission standards, location, and other particulars of 1,220 colleges.

The Princeton Review's *The Student Access Guide to the Best Colleges* by Tom Meltzer, Zachary Knover, and John Katzman. Villard Books, New York.

http:\\www.collegenet.com
This web site includes the chance to create an "Applyweb" account at the site to store your information for applications.

Visiting College Campuses by Janet Spencer and Sandra Maleson, Villard Books, New York, 1995.

APPLICATIONS

College Applications Made Easy, by Patty Marler and Jan Bailey Mattia, VGM Career Horizons, Lincolnwood, IL, 1997.

EXPENSES

See the *New York Times Magazine* of April 20, 1997 for more statistics concerning expenses.

For further information on all these funding sources, call the **College Answering Service,** 1-800-891-4599

Also see internet **http://www.salliemae.com**

FINANCIAL AID

Barron's Complete College Financing Guide, by Marguerite J. Dennis. Barron's Educational Series, Inc., Hauppauge, NY, 1995

College Check Mate: Innovative Tuition Plans that Make You a Winner, by Debra L. Wexler, Octameron Associates, Alexandria, VA, 1995

College Costs and Financing Aid Handbook, College Entrance Examination Board, New York, NY.

THE SAT* AND OTHER QUALIFYING EXAMS

Barron's How to Prepare for SAT I by Samuel C. Brownstein, Mitchel Weiner, and Sharon Weiner Green. Barron's Educational Series, Hauppauge, NY.

The College Handbook, 1996 (or latest edition), College Entrance Examination Board, New York.

Preparation for the SAT (new test), An Arco book by Macmillan, Inc.

The Princeton Review's Cracking the New SAT and PSAT by Adam Robinson and John Katzman, Villard Books, New York, NY.

PSAT / NMSQT (Covers the Preliminary SAT's and the National Merit Scholarship Qualifying Test) Barron's Educational Series.

The Very Best Coaching and Study Course for the SAT I, published by the Research and Educational Association.

ACT Cram Course, by Suzee L. Vlk, Prentice Hall, New York, NY.

Barron's Students' #1 Choice (for the) ACT (American College Testing program) by George Ehrenhaft, Robert Lehrman, Allan Mundsack, and Fred Obrecht. Barron's Educational Service, Inc., Hauppauge, NY.

DOING WELL

Toolkit for College Success by Daniel R. Walther, published by Wadsworth Publishing Company, Belmont, California. Part of the Wadsworth series of study books for college students.

PARENTS

Peterson's (of Princeton NJ) *Smart Parents Guide to College* by Ernest L. Boyer, 1996.

Peterson's web site: **http//www.petersons.com**

COMPOSITE CHART
College Questions & Answers

Use the chart on the next four pages
as your Composite College Chart of Answers.
Photocopy the chart so you can add
as many colleges as you want.

Name of College	1	2
1. Size		
2. Fees per Semester: Tuition Housing Extra costs (travel?)		
3. Distance from home/ Travel costs		
4. Competitiveness		
5. Major Options & Special programs		
6. Ave. SAT scores		
7. First reason for choosing this college and impression of reputation now		
8. Size and quality of courses		
9. Student satisfaction Housing costs		
10. Advisor availability		
11. Housing options		

3	4	5

Name of College	1	2
12. Percent commuters		
13. Financial aid possibilities		
14. Availability and reputation of fraternities and sororities on campus.		
Add any other comments here.		

3	4	5

Survey of Risk Factors That May Lead to Dropping Out

This survey is discussed in Chapter 9,
*The 4 Big Mistakes and Who Graduates,
Who Doesn't,* page 103.

Survey for Students Leaving the
University of Maryland at College Park (UMCP)

1. Where were you living while attending UMCP? (check one)
    ____(a) on campus without roommate(s)
    ____(b) on campus with roommate(s)
    ____(c) off campus in your family home.
    ____(d) off campus with non-family members.
    ____(e) off campus without roommate(s)

2. How satisfied were you with your living arrangements in general? Circle one:

1	2	3	4	5
Quite				Very
Dissatisfied				Satisfied

3. If you lived with others, how would you rate your relationship(s) with them:

1	2	3	4	5
Quite				Very
Dissatisfied				Satisfied

4. If you lived off campus, how many minutes did it usually take you to get to campus?

    _____min.

5. Were you working while attending UMCP? (check one)

    ____(a) on campus ____(b) off campus ____(c) both

    ____(d) did not work

6. If you did work, how many minutes did it usually take you to get to work? _____min.

7. If you worked, how many hours did you usually work each week? _____hrs./week

8. What percentage of your basic educational expenses (tuition, room, board, books) did you provide directly from your own earnings? _____ %

9. Did you have a declared major when you enrolled at UMCP? Yes ____. No ____. If so, what major? _____.

   Did you declare or change your major later? Yes ____. No

   ____. If so, what major?

10. What were your educational goals at the time you enrolled at UM?
    ____(a) I planned to earn a degree at UMCP.
    ____(b) I planned to take some credits, then transfer to another college.
    ____(c) I planned to take courses but was not working toward a degree.

11. Please rate your satisfaction with each of the following:

Dissatisfied	Satisfied	No opinion	
____	____	____	Orientation Program
____	____	____	Financial aid assistance
____	____	____	Registration procedures
____	____	____	Course availability
____	____	____	Counseling received for personal problems
____	____	____	Help in obtaining a part-time job
____	____	____	Career counseling
____	____	____	Residence hall facilities and environment
____	____	____	Help in finding housing off campus
____	____	____	Campus climate (prevailing attitudes and environment)

12. How many classes did you miss, on average, per week?

    a) ___ None b) ___ 1/wk c) ___ 2/wk d) ___ 4/wk

    e) ___ more than 4/wk

13. If I missed a class it was usually because: (check as many as are appropriate)
    ____(a) I was sick.
    ____(b) I had to work.
    ____(c) I slept too late for morning classes.
    ____(d) Lack of interest.
    ____(e) Transportation problems.
    ____(f) Attendance not mandatory.
    ____(g) Other _____

14. How often did you see an advisor each semester?

    a) ____ Never b) ____ 1/sem. c) ____ 2/sem. d) ___ 3/sem.
    e) ____ more than 3/sem.

    Check as many of the following as are appropriate:

    ____(a) My advisor was helpful and supportive.
    ____(b) My advisor met with me most of the times I request.
    ____(c) My advisor was not available to talk things over.
    ____(d) My advisor gave me incorrect or insufficient informa
            tion.
    ____(e) I did not have an advisor.
    ____(f) I did not try to meet with my advisor.

15. What are your immediate plans after leaving UMCP? (Check one)

    ____(a) Attend another four-year college.
            If so, what college?_____
    ____(b) Attend a community or junior college.
            If so, what college?_____
    ____(c) Work full-time (35 or more hours/week)
    ____(d) Work part-time (less than 35 hours/week)
    ____(e) Intend on returning to UMCP.
    ____(f) Not sure or Other_____.

16. The following could be factors in a student's decision to leave UMCP. Please check those reasons that you think apply to your situation.
    ____(a) Health problems.
    ____(b) I lived too far from campus.
    ____(c) Not enough time to study because I worked too many
            hours.
    ____(d) I had little chance to be involved with campus

organizations.

____(e) I was disappointed in my social life at UMCP.

____(f) Classes were too large.

____(g) I felt uncomfortable with the cultural climate at UMCP.

____(h) I did not receive an adequate orientation at UMCP.

____(i) Faculty were not available to help me/ did not know where to find help.

____(j) I could not understand my instructors or their teaching methods.

____(k) The major I wanted was not what I expected. If so, what major:_____

____(l) I could not get the courses/schedule I wanted. If so, what courses____

____(m) I could not get the major I wanted. If so, what major:_____

____(n) My overall grades were too low.

____(o) My grades in required courses were too low. Which course(s)?_____

____(p) I didn't know how to study.

____(q) I had insufficient background in mathematics.

____(r) My GPA was above 2.0, but I was not satisfied with my performance.

____(s) I don't know what I want to do and need time away from school to decide.

____(t) I received too much pressure from home for better grades.

____(u) I needed better financial assistance.

____(v) I was not earning enough credits each semester.

____(w) I took more credit hours than I could handle in some semesters.

____(x) I was too distracted by partying and other social activities.

____(y) School was too much pressure—too stressful.

____(z) Unplanned pregnancy.

____(aa) Family emergency or family obligations.

____(bb) Physical campus was difficult to negotiate (too large, insufficient parking).

____(cc) I felt discriminated against due to race, gender, religion, or sexual preference.

____(dd) I did not get along with my roommate(s).

17. Outside of class hours, how many hours did you spend on campus each day?

____(a) Almost none, If I didn't have a class I left the

campus.

_____(b) I spent a few hours a day on campus <u>between</u> classes, but I didn't stay if no class was coming up.

_____(c) I spent extra hours here, but only to study and/or to work a campus job.

_____(d) I spent one or two extra hours each day on campus with friends and activities.

_____(e) I spent <u>more than</u> two extra hours each day on campus with friends and activities.

18. Regarding alcohol, during the last three months I:

_____(a) had no alcohol.

_____(b) had an occasional drink or an occasional beer or wine.

_____(c) was intoxicated on some occasion(s).

_____(d) had some alcohol nearly every day.

19. Regarding campus social life:

_____(a) My friends were not at College Park.

_____(b) I had one or two friends at College Park.

_____(c) Most of my friends were here at College Park, but I didn't get to see them enough.

_____(d) I had many good friends at College Park and we got together frequently.

PLEASE USE THE REVERSE SIDE OF THIS PAGE FOR ADDITIONAL COMMENTS...

INDEX

M
Majors
   campus clips about 52
   changing m. and graduation
      delays 50-51
   choosing 49-52
   freshmen changing their mind
      about 33, 50
   friend's experience with 7
   on chart of answers 30-31
   number of m. 33
Management
   of money 99-100
   of schedule 60-63, 99
   of time 99
Media 3-5
Mistakes
   and relationship to dropping-
      out 103-111
   description of 93-101
   in habits 93-96
   in health 97-98
   in housing 96-97
   in management 99-100
   to avoid (Preface) x
Money
   during year off xiii-xv
   for college 9-11
   management of 99-100

N
Notes
   about the composite chart 28-
      36
   making a copy of 68-69
   necessity of 68-69
   rules for 68
   what are "good n." 69
Note cards 71-72

O
Objective tests, strategies for
      76-78
Off-To-College shower 127-128
Offers from colleges 47-49

P
Parents
   and worries 129-131
   campus clip about 128, 131
   feeling their loss 130-132
   giving off-to-college shower
      127-128
   helping son or daughter 125-
      133
   in final choice of college 126
   letter from 131
   need to know 132
   resource for 132, 139
Planning, necessity of 72-73
   for finals 80-85

R
Rationalizations for cutting
      classes 65-67
Records, keep your 100-101
   story about 100
Recommendations 44-45
   campus clip about 45
Registration
   and time management 99
   preparation for 59-63
Relationships 112-122
   conversations in 114-117
   games in 118-122
   handling problems in 103-122
Reputations of colleges 3-8, 34-
      35
   media influence on 3-8
Roommates 112-122

S
SAT and other tests 18-20
   as measure of reputation of
      the college, 4, 34
Schedules
   careful parental encourage-
      ment about 127
   campus clip about xii
   for registration 59-63
   for typical week of college 62